Especially for Mormon Missionaries

Missionaries

A meaningful collection of poems, scriptures, stories, and thoughts to inspire and aid potential, serving, and member missionaries — many never before published.

Stan & Sharon Miller and Sherm & Peg Fugal

Especially for Mormon Missionaries is published by:
Especially for Mormons, Inc.
Box 1516
American Fork, UT 84003-6516
(801) 772-0440; 0990 fax
website: www.especiallyformormons.com
email: pegfugal@aol.com

Especially for Mormon Missionaries is distributed by:
Covenant Communications, Inc.
920 East State Road/Suite F
P.O. Box 416
American Fork, UT 84003-0416
(801) 756-9966; 1049 fax

ISBN 1-57734-967-9

Copyright 2001, Especially for Mormons, Inc.
First printing: September, 2001

Other books in this series:
The Best of Especially for Mormons
Christmas Especially for Mormons

Other *Especially for Mormons* products:
The Best of Especially for Mormons on Audiocassette
The Original Five Volumes of Especially for Mormons on CD-ROM

Dedication

To our youngest sons:
Elder Michael Miller,
who, at this writing, is serving in the
Ohio Cleveland Mission
and
Elder Jeremy Fugal,
who, at this writing, is serving in the
Korea Taejon Mission,
both of whom are due to be released
at the same time this book is to be released.

Acknowledgements

As always, thanks to Stan and Sharon for the idea and help;
thanks to Sherm for the really tough work;
thanks to Randy and Maralee for designing the cover;
thanks to Tony for formatting the contents;
thanks to Paul for printing;
thanks to Jayson for directing from afar;
thanks to all of our contributors, especially Sue;
and, thanks to Covenant for distributing and marketing.

Peg Fugal, Editor
September, 2001

Forward

We are tremendously pleased with the initial response to our all-new *The Best of Especially for Mormons* and *Christmas Especially for Mormons*—released Christmas 2000.

Because the five paperback volumes of the original best-selling *Especially for Mormons* are no longer in print, the brand new, leather-like, gold-foil-stamped, hardcover editions of both *The Best of Especially for Mormons* and *Christmas Especially for Mormons* were a welcome treat to fans of the original series.

One book signing after another, Stan and I both heard the same comments:

"Oh, I love 'Especially for Mormons'."

"Oh, I'm so glad you brought it back: I don't know where my original volumes are!"

"Oh, I'm so glad you brought it back: I've loaned out the original volumes and can't remember who has them."

"Oh, I love the new hardcover: my paperback volumes are in shreds."

"Oh, I love the fact that you picked the best stories for me so I don't have to search all five volumes anymore."

"Oh, I need 'The Best of' for my kids who never did get the five original volumes."

"Oh, I love the new design."

"Oh, I love having all the Christmas stories in one book."

Of course, some people have never even heard of *Especially for Mormons*, let alone the two new comeback volumes—but, then, with one leaf through, they, too, became fans.

The Best of was **not** written for the old fans of *Especially for Mormons*: it was written for everyone who has grown up and left home—and *Especially for Mormons* behind on Mom's and Dad's bookshelves—or joined the church since and needs *The Best of* in their own church library for inspiration, family home evening, church lessons, and sacrament talks. If you have family or friends who fall into that category, then please give *The Best of* to them; they will treasure it.

Christmas Especially for Mormons was even better received—in fact, it out-sold *The Best of*. No matter how often fans quizzed or tried to trip up Stan and me at book-signings, they always, always, always found their all-time favorite Christmas story in *Christmas Especially for Mormons*.

Another surprise was fans' response to *The Original Five Volumes of Especially for Mormons on CD-ROM*—produced by Covenant Communications, Inc.—and the only way one can now access the original five volumes. The CD also includes all four sets of scriptures, with a powerful search engine for recalling any topic from any volume, along with corresponding scriptures.

The Best of Especially for Mormons is also available on audiocassette, also from Covenant.

We want to thank Covenant for their support in developing and marketing the new *Especially for Mormons* products. Their insight into the market as well as their invaluable resources turned what could have been a nightmare into a great pleasure. We are grateful, too, for all the LDS bookstores, particularly Seagull Book and Tape and Deseret Book, for retailing new *Especially for Mormons* products. Most of all, we are grateful to LDS readers everywhere who helped make the original *Especially for Mormons,* as well as the new *The Best of* and *Christmas* volumes such tremendous successes.

Now, allow me to explain the brilliance behind this, our best book so far. When I first started, I had only a handful of missionary pieces from the previous volumes. I had a lot of work ahead of me. I started writing my own stories—while simultaneously emailing everyone I know, asking for their stories—who emailed everyone they knew—until we had a brilliant collection of missionary stories. Then, I started searching the scriptures for the best missionary scriptures and stories. I personally scanned the Book of Mormon twice. My favorite section of this book is **"The Eight Great Book of Mormon Missionaries"**, found on pages 41-84. We are all vaguely familiar with their stories—which are scattered all over the Book of Mormon. No more. I have collected all eight stories, into one chronological set, with subtitles, for ease and fun in reading. It is my greatest effort herein. Enjoy and pass on.

An interesting thing happened to me while I was writing for and editing *Especially for Mormon Missionaries.* I had been suffering from a personal tragedy for many months. I had never been so down, so discouraged, so rudderless. I was beginning to wonder if the malaise would ever lift. It did. The minute I began recalling and writing my own missionary stories and editing others. I experienced a spiritual uplift that I both needed and had not enjoyed in a very long time. I know this book will have the same effect on you and the missionaries in your life.

Our fourth volume, *Especially for Mormon Women*, will be released Christmas 2002. We invite you to submit pieces you would like to see included by simply emailing the piece to me at pegfugal@aol.com anytime before the end of July 2002. (I am sorry, but we cannot accept material in any other way.)

Peg Fugal, Editor
September, 2001

Table of Contents

Poems

Courage, My Son

Courage, my son, and don't forget,
That God is with you in every step.

You take for him in a righteous cause,
Such as teaching his sacred and holy laws.

There are souls out there waiting to hear
The message you carry of faith and prayer.

Of a God who dwells in the heavens above,
And rules the world with the spirit of love.

Forget all worries and earthly care,
And put your soul in the message you bear.

—Lula Anderson

Be Not Discouraged

Discouragement is always the devil's tool,
But show him quickly that you are no fool.

Get down on your knees in humble prayer:
God's encouraging Spirit will meet you there.

There are souls out there in the mist and fog,
Who are waiting for you and your message from God.

For he has love for each child that he owns,
And wants them back in his heavenly home.

Be not discouraged, no matter how hard the way,
But deliver the message God wants you to say.

The Lord, My Companion, and Me

The Lord, my companion, and me,
Are a great combination, we three;
For where he would lead us, we go willingly,
The Lord, my companion, and me.

The Lord, my companion, and me,
Have a work that is endless, you see.
For the good, honest souls must be gathered, we're told
By the Lord, my companion, and me.

The Lord, my companion, and me
Must pull as a team, constantly.
If we would have power, we will remember each hour:
It's the Lord first, my companion, then me.

Free Wheeling

I have often wondered
As the weeks go by,
How my footsteps were guided
From time to time.

Who turned the wheel
When I knew not why,
And took me away
From the way I planned.

Who led me up
To an unknown door,
With a familiar message,
"Would you like to know more?"

Today came the mail,
With letters of cheer,
From friends and relatives
Far and near.

I read them all
And then I knew:
For each one ended,
"We pray for you."

—*Zelma Miller*

Today, I Planted

Today,
I planted a seed of truth
In fertile soil;
Now, I wait,
Through the soft rain
Of man's inherent goodness,
And the warm sun
Of eternal love,
For a sign of growth;
And pray,
That strong roots support
The first tender shoots,
And bear testimony
That it may flourish,
And wax strong,
And blossom,
And spill its own seed
Again into fertile soil.

My Reward

A lady said to me one day,
You're very foolish, I must say,
To leave your home and friends you love,
And, for no wage, preach God above.

Our Pastors get a salary great,
The gospel truths to promulgate;
You come out for two years' time,
And don't receive a single dime.

That's true, I said, I don't get paid,
As your Pastors do, in temporal aid;
My ransom is the joy sublime
That fills my soul at even time.

When I have tried with one accord
To spread the gospel of my Lord,
The chance to serve means more to me
Than all the wealth the world can see.

To My Mormon Elder

You will never know of the gladness you brought
To a heart overburdened with care,
Of the beautiful, wonderful changes you wrought
In a life once so pitifully bare.

You will never know that you brought Christ so near,
Who had once seemed so far, far away,
That you gave him to me as a big brother so dear,
Whom I understand now when I pray.

And, I'll never know of others whose lives
You've brightened just as you have mine,
Of many a soul who now hopefully strives
With Jesus for a comrade divine.

But our Heavenly Father who watches will know
And will nurture each seed that you've sown,
That, when harvest time comes in the fields here below,
He may gather sheaves for his own.

And, when he has called you, your record to share
On that glorious beautiful day,
You'll find souls that are faithful and hearts that are true
Because you have journeyed this way.

❧

Loving a Missionary

Loving a missionary isn't all play,
The life it demands of you isn't so gay.

It's mostly the having, but not to hold,
It's being too young and feeling so old.

It's a life of skimmed milk—without any cream,
And being in love with a wonderful dream.

Yes, loving your missionary means "Good-bye" at the plane,
And two years must pass before you see him again.

You reluctantly, painfully let him go,
While you are aching inside for wanting him so.

Then you wait for his word that everything's well,
And bide through a miserable letterless spell.

Then comes the mail, you are giddy with joy,
And you pounce like a child with a shiny new toy.

You realize that he is so far away,
And your love for him grows greater each day.

You are proud of the job he is helping to do,
And you know he is doing it, thinking of you.

Loving a missionary is undefined fears,
And crying at night till there aren't any tears.

Then seeking comfort, you kneel down to pray,
And put your whole heart in the words that you say.

And you find that your feet are on the sand and not sod,
And your source of strength comes only from God.

&

Prayer for a Missionary

Father in heaven,
Hear this my plea,
For I have a loved one
In service to thee.

Give him the wisdom
To know what to do,
Give him the courage
To stand for what's true.

Develop his faith,
So he'll always pray
To thee for guidance
From day to day.

Keep him forever
Safe from all harm,
That we at home
Will be free from alarm.

Give him the strength
To escape every snare,
Overcome all temptation,
Be free from all care.

Give him patience
To understand
The customs and people
Of a strange land.

Let him radiate love
That he may be
Able to turn
Many hearts unto thee.

And let him know
That I wait cheerfully
For that glorious day
Thou returnest him to me.

—Janelle Smith

The Reason Why

I tried and failed in every way
To find a soul to teach someday.
After a long week, I had toiled
To find my work had all been foiled.
At last, I finally knelt in prayer
And said, "0h, Lord it isn't fair
That I should work so hard for you
And yet my people all fall through.

"I've come out here for two long years
And endured hardships and overcome fears.
I've preached the gospel with all my might
From early morning till late at night.

"All these rules I've applied,
Yet, everything has failed that I have tried.
0h, Lord, you know I'm working hard;
Isn't it about time I got my reward?
Please tell me what I should do
That I might be able to satisfy you."

The answer came to me
And set my mind and conscience free.

He said, "My son, it's the same old story:
Your eyes are not single to my glory.
The reason you have tried in vain
Is because you are trying to build your fame.
The reason I have let you fail
Is because you let your pride prevail,
I've let you wander in the dark and fumble
Because I'm trying to make you humble.
And the reason your people all fall through
Is because your work is not true.

"My son, I'm afraid you're just a fake;
You're not baptizing for my sake.
You think of numbers ten by ten
To raise your stature in the eyes of men.
You're thinking only of your own success
And that type of person I will not bless.
Your actions and your thoughts are before my eyes.
I'll never give my blessings to you
Until your heart is pure and true."

I knelt in prayer and said to him,
"Oh, Lord, forgive me for this sin.
What a fool I've been to surmise
That my thoughts were hidden from your eyes.
You won't let divine blessings impart
To satisfy the lusts of my evil heart.
I'm thankful you revealed this unto me;
My eyes were blind, but now I see.
Oh, Lord, I'm really a foolish man,
Without your help I can't work your plan.
Remove from my heart that awful greed
And help me to plant that fertile seed.
From this time on, let it be
That my labors are directed only to thee."

To a Missionary at Christmastime

I know it can get lonely
Away from home at Christmas time,
And that your thoughts must wander,
Longing for that homey clime.

You think of all the folks back home,
You wonder what fun's brewing;
You gaze at your girl's photograph
And wonder what she's doing.

A gentle tugging at your heart
Tells you you're far away
From the familiar hearth
That has kept you safe from the fray.

But you, my dearest elder,
Are the most blessed of us all,
For you've a special Christmas; yes,
You've a certain call.

For you and only you can give
The greatest Christmas gift—
A gift that's sent straight from God
To saddened hearts uplift.

Yes, it is the choicest gift,
This Christmas gift you're giving,
The gift of truth, of faith in God,
That makes our life worth living.

❧

Have You Been a Missionary?

Have you ever preached a sermon with an awful stomach ache?
And your head so full of throbbing that you thought it soon would break?
Have you ever read your Bible under shelter of some tree,
While the rain fell all around you till it formed a little sea?

Have you ever sailed six miles to bless a member's baby?
Have you eaten a Christmas dinner made of common spuds and gravy?
Have you ever tried to twist your tongue around another country's lingo,
And said, "I'll learn this language yet, if it's the last thing I do, by jingo!"?

Have you ever tried to bring comfort to a family rent with pain?
Have you told a crying mother that her son would live again?
Have you ever watched jeering eyes as you preached upon the street?
Have you ever thrilled with unbound joy when with some interest you chanced to meet?

Did you ever feel the least bit slighted because someone forgot to write?
Did you ever think, "She'll never wait, but, then again, she might"?
Did you ever come home discouraged after preaching had gone wrong?
Did you ever change your feeling just by singing a happy song?

If you've hiked along the highway, if you have stood in the rain,
If you've preached on an empty stomach without a thought of gain,
If you've been discouraged, if you have seen the work go contrary,
If you've done these things and laughed, my friend, then you've been a missionary!

The Best Two Years of My Life

Taking a bath in cold water with a spoon
And trudging up five flights of stairs,
Trying to digest my companion's home cooking,
And thinking nobody cares.

Are these the best two years of my life?
Surely, it's got to get better.
If these are the best two years of my life,
Then, at least, can't I get just one letter?

Keeping appointments where no one shows up,
And sitting around on the floor,
Mosquitoes eating my face and my feet,
And being too tall for the door.

Are you sure these are the best two years of my life?
I miss all my family and friends;
If these are the best two years of my life,
Why can't I wait till it ends?

Eating my fill of strange foreign food,
And taking my shots for malaria,
Having another door slammed in my face,
While I'm trying to calm Mom's hysteria.

Are these really the best two years of my life?
Are you sure I'm going to live through it?
If these are the best two years of my life,
I'd better get busy and get to it.

Then watching a person's life change for the better,
And teaching of God's great love and care;
Then hearing his halting, humble attempt
To offer his first simple prayer.

Oh, these are the best two years of my life!
They couldn't possibly get any better!
I'm happy, I'm fine, I'm doing just great,
So please disregard my last letter!

—*Susan Hiatt Biggs*

Hungry Spirit

She gently turned the pages,
Warmed by words of truth;
With hungry spirit,
Knelt to ask (as Joseph knelt),
Seeking light, expecting affirmation.

She cast her searchings
On this new-found God,
Looked heavenward, and listened.

Then, as Joseph Smith beheld,
As Moroni did reveal,
The light of truth descended,
A sacred knowledge,
Within her grasp.

She traveled as with Nephi,
Beheld the promised land,
Felt the spirit of prophecy
As Abinidi stood before the king
And called him to repent.

She heard the things that Alma taught
And saw the wars and wickedness.
She saw the Lord extend his hand,
Protect those who were faithful,
And bless them in his mercy.

Oh, sweet revelation,
A history saved at Moroni's hand.
Translated by the gift of God,
That all might have that certain faith,
A testimony in wisdom's light.

She walked into waters of baptism,
Compelled by sacred history
To stand uprightly before the Lord.

A convert to concepts redeeming,
Her thirsting soul refreshed,
Her hungry spirit fed.

—Suzanne Dean

∽

In His Steps

"The road is rough," I said, "dear Lord;
These stones, they hurt me so."
He said, "Dear child, I understand;
I walked it long ago."

"But there's a cool green path," I said,
"I'll walk there for a time."
"No child," he gently answered me.
"The green road does not climb."

"My burden, Lord, is far to great,
How can I bear it so?"
"My child," said he, "I know its weight;
I bore my cross, you know."

"I wish there were some friends with me,
Who'd make my way their own."
"Ah, yes," he said, "Gethsemane
Was hard to face alone."

And so I climbed the stony path,
Content at last to know,
That where my Master had not gone,
I would not need to go.

And strangely then I found new friends,
The burden grew less sore,
As I remembered—long ago,
He went this way before.

—*Leona B.Gates*

❧

Highs and Lows

A mission is strange experience,
A trial and a test,
A mission throws at you the worst,
Yet, teaches you the best.

I've never been so happy,
I've never been so depressed,
I've never felt so forsaken,
I've never been so blessed.

I've never been so confused,
Things have never been so clear,
I've never felt my Heavenly Father so distant,
He's never been so near.

I've never been so discouraged,
I've never been so full of hope,
I feel I could go on forever,
I've come to the end of my rope.

I've never had it quite so easy,
I've never had it quite so tough,
Things have never been so smooth,
Things have never been so rough.

I've never been through such a deep valley,
I've never been to so high a peak,
I've never felt so sure and strong,
I've never felt so weak.

I never had so many ups,
I've never had so many downs,
I've never had so many smiles,
I've never had so many frowns.

I've never been so lonely,
I've never had so many friends.
Boy! I hope this is over soon!
Gosh! I hope it never ends!

❧

The "Black Name Tag"

The "Black Name Tag" upon my chest,
We are the men, the church's best;
Some may boast, some may brag,
But only a few wear the "Black Name Tag"!

Twenty-four months without a date,
But we are tough, we can wait;
Our girls sit home, they'll never brag,
That their brave men wear the "Black Name Tag"!

Back at home our girls wait,
But not for long, she starts to date;
Her interest soon begins to lag,
She "Dear Johns" the "Black Name Tag"!

We return home, we resume life,
Start our search to find a wife;
But finds are few and efforts sag,
Such is life for the "Black Name Tag"!

You find a fox, she has a man,
You find a chick, she has a plan;
You find the one, but what a drag,
'Cause now she wears the "Black Name Tag"!

(even more fun when sung to the tune of the '60s hit, "The Green Beret")

❧

Gospel Pills

If you want to be happy the rest of your life,
And never suffer from spiritual ills,
You must follow some rules of our Heavenly Father,
They are known as gospel prin-ci-pills.

The Ten Commandments and the Articles of Faith,
Are the most basic "pills" of all;

The Word of Wisdom keeps our bodies clean,
It will help us grow big and tall.

Our priesthood "pills" run the Church,
The same as in days of old;
But, without the scriptures and missionaries,
The stories would never get told.

Love and service "pills" go hand-in-hand,
As do fasting and prayer;
All symptoms vanish as we partake,
And we feel Heavenly Father near.

As we pay tithing—it's only a tenth—
Blessings come and we're safe from harm;
And taking the sacrament every week,
Gives us a real "shot in the arm".

So we may return to our Father in Heaven,
A wonderful plan he's designed;
With Jesus as Savior and ordinances, too,
Our way back to Father we'll find.

Our faith increases each time that we,
Partake of a "prin-ci-pill";
As we receive the recommended daily allowance,
Our spiritual vessel is filled.

—Davis, Utah LDS Seminary

Which Life Do I Want?

As I stare out the window,
Tears still in my eyes,
I see the vision of those I love,
As we said our last good-byes.

The flight was long and tiring,
As two questions plagued my mind:
Do I want the life that's ahead of me,
Or the one I left behind?

You see twenty-four months is such a long time,
For going door to door;
In my reflection, I thought,
There must be something more.

I struggled down off the plane,
Looking for a friendly face;
When a man called President said,
"Son, you've come to the right place!"

I sit reflecting once again,
As this day is my last,
Please, Lord, it isn't fair,
The time went way too fast.

As I stare out the window,
Tears still in my eyes,
I see the visions of those I love,
As we said our last good-byes.

The flight was long and tiring,
As two questions plagued my mind:
Do I want the life that's ahead of me,
Or the one I left behind?

❧

How Great Shall Be Your Joy

The work was hard in olden days with no purse or script;
Today we've cars and planes and ships, but still the same old "sticks".

Sometimes it's hard to keep enthused—with the work I mean;
Sometimes it seems as though we're hot, then cold, then in between.

Remembrance is what we need—of why we're really here;
How much better that would be, because then we'd have no fear.

The Lord, his hand is always there: he leads us day to day;
In fact, he takes us to the people who really want "the way".

He blesses us with health and strength and gives us all we need;
He tells us when and what to say and how to plant "the seed".

"How great shall be your joy" is more than just a thought;
When someone you have loved and taught has found the truth they've sought.
                                                    —*Filip Askerland*

❧

Baptism

From amidst the mass of human life, are those who desire the truth;
Searching, searching, in hopes of a fuller light and truth.

The skies grow dark and gloom draws in, but there rises a light in the mist;
Which comes in twos with white shirts and shoes and a pair of scripture in fist.

A searching soul with high ideals desires their zeal and invites them in;
And then heeds the counsel and guidance they share from deep, deep within.

Restoration and progression, prophets, revelation, and what is truth;
Commandments and obedience and Christ's relationship to you.

As a flower grows from a very small seed, the testimony begins to bloom;
Though faced with setbacks and tests of strength, the truth fills all the room.

The decision is made, the baptism is layed, and happiness in the air;
For the gate is opened and the soul steps in to the happiness of those who
are there.

Christ set the example that we must follow and the truth of his humble way;
That we may fulfill the calling he gave to return to him someday.

—Reed Markham

Scriptures

Nephi: The Secret of His Success

1 Nephi 2

16 And it came to pass that I, Nephi, being exceedingly young, nevertheless being large in stature, and also having *great desires to know of the mysteries of God,* wherefore, *I did cry unto the Lord; and behold he did visit me, and did soften my heart that I did believe all the words which had been spoken by my father; wherefore, I did not rebel against him like unto my brothers.*

∽

The Four Sons of Mosiah: The Secret of Their Success

Alma 17

1 And now it came to pass that as Alma was journeying from the land of Gideon southward, away to the land of Manti, behold, to his astonishment, he met with the sons of Mosiah journeying towards the land of Zarahemla.

2 *Now these sons of Mosiah were with Alma at the time the angel first appeared unto him;* therefore Alma did rejoice exceedingly to see his brethren; and what added more to his joy, *they were still his brethren in the Lord;* yea, and *they had waxed strong in the knowledge of the truth; for they were men of a sound understanding and they had searched the scriptures diligently, that they might know the word of God.*

3 But this is not all; they had *given themselves to much prayer, and fasting; therefore they had the spirit of prophecy, and the spirit of revelation, and when they taught, they taught with power and authority of God.*

4 And they had been teaching the word of God for the space of fourteen years among the Lamanites, having had much success in bringing many to the knowledge of the truth; yea, *by the power of their words many were brought before the altar of God,* to call on his name and confess their sins before him.

5 Now these are the circumstances which attended them in their journeyings, for *they had many afflictions; they did suffer much, both in body and in mind, such as hunger, thirst and fatigue, and also much labor in the spirit.*

6 Now these were their journeyings: Having taken leave of their father, Mosiah, in the first year of the judges; having *refused the kingdom which their father was desirous to confer upon them,* and also this was the minds of the people;

7 Nevertheless they departed out of the land of Zarahemla, and took their swords, and their spears, and their bows, and their arrows, and their slings; and this they did that they might *provide food for themselves* while in the wilderness.

8 And thus they departed into the wilderness with their numbers which they had selected, to go up to the land of Nephi, to preach the word of God unto the Lamanites.

9 And it came to pass that they *journeyed many days in the wilderness, and they fasted much and prayed much that the Lord would grant unto them a portion of his Spirit to go with them, and abide with them, that they might be an instrument in the hands of God to bring, if it were possible, their brethren, the Lamanites, to the knowledge of the truth, to the knowledge of the baseness of the traditions of their fathers, which were not correct.*

10 And it came to pass that the *Lord did visit them with his Spirit,* and said unto them: Be comforted. And they were comforted.

11 And the Lord said unto them also: Go forth among the Lamanites, thy brethren, and establish my word; yet ye shall *be patient in long-suffering and afflictions, that ye may show forth good examples unto them in me, and I will make an instrument of thee in my hands unto the salvation of many souls.*

12 And it came to pass that *the hearts of the sons of Mosiah, and also those who were with them, took courage to go forth unto the Lamanites to declare unto them the word of God.*

13 And it came to pass when they had arrived in the borders of the land of the Lamanites, that they separated themselves and departed one from another, *trusting in the Lord that they should meet again at the close of their harvest; for they supposed that great was the work which they had undertaken.*

14 And assuredly it was great, *for they had undertaken to preach the word of God to a wild and a hardened and a ferocious people;* a people who delighted in murdering the Nephites, and robbing and plundering them; and their hearts were set upon riches, or upon gold and silver, and precious stones; yet they sought to obtain these things by murdering and plundering, that they might not labor for them with their own hands.

15 Thus they were a very indolent people, many of whom did worship idols, and the curse of God had fallen upon them because of the traditions of their fathers; notwithstanding the promises of the Lord were extended unto them on the conditions of repentance.

16 Therefore, *this was the cause for which the sons of Mosiah had undertaken the work, that perhaps they might bring them unto repentance; that perhaps they might bring them to know the plan of redemption.*

17 Therefore *they separated themselves one from another, and went forth among them, every man alone, according to the word and power of God which was given unto him.*

Captain Moroni: The Secret of His Success

Alma 48

11 And Moroni was a strong and a mighty man; he was a man of a perfect understanding; yea, a man that did not delight in bloodshed; a man whose soul did joy in the liberty and the freedom of his country, and his brethren from bondage and slavery;

12 Yea, a man whose heart did swell with thanksgiving to his God, for the many privileges and blessings which he bestowed upon his people; a man who did labor exceedingly for the welfare and safety of his people.

13 Yea, and he was a man who was firm in the faith of Christ, and he had sworn with an oath to defend his people, his rights, and his country, and his religion, even to the loss of his blood.

14 Now the Nephites were taught to defend themselves against their enemies, even to the shedding of blood if it were necessary; yea, and they were also taught never to give an offense, yea, and never to raise the sword except it were against an enemy, except it were to preserve their lives.

15 And this was their faith, that by so doing God would prosper them in the land, or in other words, if they were faithful in keeping the commandments of God that he would prosper them in the land; yea, warn them to flee, or to prepare for war, according to their danger;

16 And also, that God would make it known unto them whither they should go to defend themselves against their enemies, and by so doing, the Lord would deliver them; and *this was the faith of Moroni, and his heart did glory in it; not in the shedding of blood but in doing good, in preserving his people, yea, in keeping the commandments of God, yea, and resisting iniquity.*

17 Yea, verily, verily I say unto you, *if all men had been, and were, and ever would be, like unto Moroni, behold, the very powers of hell would have been shaken forever; yea, the devil would never have power over the hearts of the children of men.*

18 Behold, *he was a man like unto Ammon, the son of Mosiah, yea, and even the other sons of Mosiah, yea, and also Alma and his sons, for they were all men of God.*

❧

The Defining Characteristics of the Prophet Joseph Smith

1. He had an unchanging faith and trust in God

2. He loved the truth

3. He was humble

4. He loved his fellowman

—*John A. Widtsoe*

❧

Old Testament Prophets on Missionary Work

Isaiah

And many people shall go and say, Come ye, and let us go up to the mountain of the LORD, to the house of the God of Jacob; *and he will teach us of his ways,* and we will walk in his paths: for out of Zion shall go forth the law, and the word of the LORD from Jerusalem.

—Isaiah 2:3

And he said, It is a light thing that thou shouldest be my servant to raise up the tribes of Jacob, and to restore the preserved of Israel: *I will also give thee for a light to the Gentiles,* that thou mayest be my salvation unto the end of the earth.

—Isaiah 49:6

How beautiful upon the mountains are the feet of him that bringeth good tidings, *that publisheth peace;* that bringeth good tidings of good, that publisheth salvation; that saith unto Zion, Thy God reigneth!

—Isaiah 52:7

The Spirit of the Lord GOD [is] upon me; because *the LORD hath anointed me to preach good tidings* unto the meek; he hath sent me to bind up the brokenhearted, to proclaim liberty to the captives, and the opening of the prison to [them that are] bound;

—Isaiah 61:1

ॐ

Jeremiah

Turn, O backsliding children, saith the LORD; for I am married unto you: and I will take you *one of a city, and two of a family, and I will bring you to Zion:*

—Jeremiah 3:14

Behold, *I will send for many fishers,* saith the LORD, and they shall fish them; and after will I send for many hunters, and they shall hunt them from every mountain, and from every hill, and out of the holes of the rocks.

—Jeremiah 16:6

ॐ

Ezekiel

For thus saith the Lord GOD; Behold, I, [even] *I, will both search my sheep, and seek them out.*

—Ezekiel 34:11

ॐ

Jonah

Arise, *go to Nineveh, that great city, and cry against it;* for their wickedness is come up before me.

—Jonah 1:2

Arise, go unto Nineveh, that great city, and *preach* unto it *the preaching that I bid thee.*

—Jonah 3:2

❧

New Testament Prophets on Missionary Work

Matthew

And he saith unto them, Follow me, and *I will make you fishers of men.*

—Matthew 4:19

Whosoever therefore shall break one of these least commandments, and shall teach men so, he shall be called the least in the kingdom of heaven: but *whosoever shall do and teach [them],* the same shall be called great in the kingdom of heaven.

—Matthew 5:19

But *go rather to the lost sheep of the house of Israel.*

—Matthew 10:6

And it came to pass, when Jesus had made an end of commanding his twelve disciples, *he departed thence to teach and to preach* in their cities.

—Matthew 11:1

And this *gospel* of the kingdom *shall be preached in all the world* for a witness unto all nations; and then shall the end come.

—Matthew 24:14

Go ye therefore, and *teach all nations, baptizing them* in the name of the Father, and of the Son, and of the Holy Ghost:

—Matthew 28:19

❧

Mark

John did baptize in the wilderness, and *preach the baptism of repentance for the remission of sins.*

—Mark 1:4

And he ordained twelve, that they should be with him, and *that he might send them forth to preach,*

—Mark 3:14

And he said unto them, Go ye into all the world, and *preach the gospel to every creature*.

—*Mark 16:15*

Luke

And he sent *them to preach the kingdom of God*, and to heal the sick.

—*Luke 9:2*

After these things the Lord appointed other *seventy* also, and *sent them two and two before his face* into every city and place, whither he himself would come.

—*Luke 10:1*

But I have prayed for thee, that thy faith fail not: and *when thou art converted, strengthen thy brethren*.

—*Luke 22:32*

And *ye are witnesses of these things*.

—*Luke 24:48*

John

Say not ye, There are yet four months, and [then] cometh harvest? behold, I say unto you, Lift up your eyes, and look on the *fields*; for they *are white already to harvest*.

—*John 4:35*

Ye have not chosen me, but I have chosen you, and ordained you, that ye should *go and bring forth fruit*, and [that] your fruit should remain: that whatsoever ye shall ask of the Father in my name, he may give it you.

—*John 15:16*

He saith unto him the third time, Simon, [son] of Jonas, lovest thou me? Peter was grieved because he said unto him the third time, Lovest thou me? And he said unto him, Lord, thou knowest all things; thou knowest that I love thee. Jesus saith unto him, *Feed my sheep*.

—*John 21:17*

Acts

And daily in the temple, and in every house, *they ceased not to teach and preach* Jesus Christ.

—*Acts 5:42*

But when they *believed Philip preaching the things concerning the kingdom* of God, and the name of Jesus Christ, they were baptized, both men and women.

—Acts 8:12

And he *commanded us to preach unto the people,* and to testify that it is he which was ordained of God [to be] the Judge of quick and dead.

—Acts 10:42

And *Paul,* as his manner was, went in unto them, and three sabbath days *reasoned with them out of the scriptures.*

—Acts 17:2

❧

Romans

And *how shall they preach, except they be sent?* as it is written, How beautiful are the feet of them that preach the gospel of peace, and bring glad tidings of good things!

—Romans 10:15

❧

1 Corinthians

But *we preach Christ crucified,* unto the Jews a stumblingblock, and unto the Greeks foolishness;

—I Corinthians 1:23

For though I preach the gospel, I have nothing to glory of: for necessity is laid upon me; yea, *woe is unto me, if I preach not the gospel!*

—1 Corinthians 9:16

Moreover, brethren, *I declare unto you the gospel* which I preached unto you, which also ye have received, and wherein ye stand;

—1 Corinthians 15:1

❧

2 Corinthians

For *we preach not ourselves, but Christ* Jesus the Lord; and ourselves your servants for Jesus' sake.

—2 Corinthians 4:5

❧

2 Timothy

Preach the word; be instant in season, out of season; reprove, rebuke, exhort with all longsuffering and doctrine.

—2 Timothy 4:2

ॐ

Revelation

And I saw *another angel* fly in the midst of heaven, *having the everlasting gospel to preach* unto them that dwell on the earth, and to every nation, and kindred, and tongue, and people,

—Revelation 14:6

ॐ

Book of Mormon Prophets on Missionary Work

Jacob

And we did magnify our office unto the Lord, taking upon us the responsibility, answering the sins of the people upon our own heads if we did not *teach them the word of God with all diligence;* wherefore, by laboring with our might their blood might not come upon our garments; otherwise their blood would come upon our garments, and we would not be found spotless at the last day.

—Jacob 1:19

ॐ

Mosiah

And it came to pass that after the space of two years that Abinadi came among them in disguise, that they knew him not, and began to prophesy among them, saying: Thus has the Lord commanded me, saying—Abinadi, go and *prophesy unto this my people,* for they have hardened their hearts against my words; they have repented not of their evil doings; therefore, I will visit them in my anger, yea, in my fierce anger will I visit them in their iniquities and abominations.

—Mosiah 12:1

And *these are they* who have published peace, who have brought good tidings of good, *who have published salvation;* and said unto Zion: Thy God reigneth!

—Mosiah 15:14

Yea, and are willing to mourn with those that mourn; yea, and comfort those that stand in need of comfort, and to *stand as witnesses of God at all times* and in all things, and in all places that ye may be in, even until death, that ye may be redeemed of God, and be numbered with those of the first resurrection, that ye may have eternal life—

—Mosiah 18:19

ॐ

Alma

And they had been teaching the word of God for the space of fourteen years among the Lamanites, having had much success in *bringing many to the knowledge of the truth;* yea, by the power of their words many were brought before the altar of God, to call on his name and confess their sins before him.

—*Alma 17:4*

But this is not all; for he *expounded unto them the plan of redemption,* which was prepared from the foundation of the world; and he also made known unto them concerning the coming of Christ, and all the works of the Lord did he make known unto them.

—*Alma 18:39*

For behold, the *Lord doth grant unto all nations,* of their own nation and tongue, *to teach his word,* yea, in wisdom, all that he seeth fit that they should have; therefore we see that the Lord doth counsel in wisdom, according to that which is just and true.

—*Alma 29:8*

❧

The Lord on Missionary Work
(from the Doctrine and Covenants)

And they shall *go forth and none shall stay them,* for I the Lord have commanded them.

—*D&C 1:5*

That the fulness of my *gospel might be proclaimed by the weak and the simple* unto the ends of the world, and before kings and rulers.

—*D&C 1:23*

Now behold, a *marvelous work is about to come forth* among the children of men.

—*D&C 4:1*

Seek not to *declare my word, but first seek to obtain my word,* and then shall your tongue be loosed; then, if you desire, you shall have my Spirit and my word, yea, the power of God unto the convincing of men.

—*D&C 11:21*

And now, behold, I say unto you, that the thing which will be of the *most worth unto you will be to declare repentance* unto this people, that you may bring souls unto me, that you may rest with them in the kingdom of my Father. Amen.

—*D&C 15:6*

And if it so be that you should labor all your days in crying repentance unto this people, and *bring, save it be one soul unto me, how great shall be your joy* with him in the kingdom of my Father!

—*D&C 18:15*

And ye are called to bring to pass the gathering of mine elect; for *mine elect hear my voice and harden not their hearts;*

—*D&C 29:7*

Open your mouths and they shall be filled, and you shall become even as Nephi of old, who journeyed from Jerusalem in the wilderness.

—*D&C 33:8*

And there are *none* that *doeth good except those who are ready to receive the fulness of my gospel,* which I have sent forth unto this generation.

—*D&C 35:12*

That as many as shall come before my servants Sidney Rigdon and Joseph Smith, Jun., embracing this calling and commandment, shall be *ordained and sent forth to preach* the everlasting gospel among the nations—

—*D&C 36:5*

And inasmuch as my people shall assemble themselves at the Ohio, I have kept in store a blessing such as is not known among the children of men, and it shall be poured forth upon their heads. And *from thence men shall go forth into all nations.*

—*D&C 39:15*

And ye shall *go forth* in the power of my Spirit, *preaching my gospel, two by two,* in my name, lifting up your voices as with the sound of a trump, declaring my word like unto angels of God.

—*D&C 42:6*

Again I say unto you, that it shall *not* be given to any one to go forth to *preach my gospel,* or to build up my church, *except he be ordained* by some one who has authority, and it is known to the church that he has authority and has been regularly ordained by the heads of the church.

—*D&C 42:11*

Again I say, hearken ye elders of my church, whom I have appointed: Ye are not sent forth to be taught, but to *teach the children of men* the things which I have put into your hands by the power of my Spirit;

—*D&C 43:15*

Wherefore, I give unto you a commandment that ye *go among this people, and say unto them,* like unto mine apostle of old, whose name was Peter:

—*D&C 49:11*

Verily I say unto you, he that is ordained of me and *sent forth to preach the word of truth* by the Comforter, in the Spirit of truth, doth he preach it by the Spirit of truth or some other way?

—*D&C 50:17*

And let them *journey together, or two by two,* as seemeth them good, only let my servant Reynolds Cahoon, and my servant Samuel H. Smith, with whom I am well pleased, be not separated until they return to their homes, and this for a wise purpose in me.

—D&C 61:35

And then you may return to bear record, yea, even altogether, or two by two, as seemeth you good, it mattereth not unto me; only be faithful, and *declare glad tidings unto the inhabitants* of the earth, or among the congregations of the wicked.

—D&C 62:5

And again, verily I say unto you, *those who desire in their hearts,* in meekness, *to warn sinners* to repentance, let them be ordained unto this power.

—D&C 63:57

Behold, thus saith the Lord unto you my servants Joseph Smith, Jun., and Sidney Rigdon, that the time has verily come that it is necessary and expedient in me that you should *open your mouths in proclaiming my gospel,* the things of the kingdom, expounding the mysteries thereof out of the scriptures, according to that portion of Spirit and power which shall be given unto you, even as I will.

—D&C 71:1

Lifting up your voices as with the sound of a trump, *proclaiming the truth according to the revelations* and commandments which I have given you.

—D&C 75:4

For I will forgive you of your sins with this commandment—that you remain steadfast in your minds in solemnity and the spirit of prayer, in *bearing testimony to all the world* of those things which are communicated unto you.

—D&C 84:61

Behold, *I send you out to reprove the world* of all their unrighteous deeds, and to teach them of a judgment which is to come.

—D&C 84:87

Behold, I sent you out to testify and warn the people, and it becometh *every man who hath been warned to warn his neighbor.*

—D&C 88:81

For it shall come to pass in that day, that *every man shall hear the fulness of the gospel in his own tongue,* and in his own language, through those who are ordained unto this power, by the administration of the Comforter, shed forth upon them for the revelation of Jesus Christ.

—D&C 90:11

For *it shall be given you* in the very hour, yea, in the very moment, *what ye shall say.*

—D&C 100:6

The *Seventy are also called to preach* the gospel, and to be especial witnesses unto the Gentiles and in all the world—thus differing from other officers in the church in the duties of their calling.

—D&C 107:25

For there are many yet on the earth among all sects, parties, and denominations, who are blinded by the subtle craftiness of men, whereby they lie in wait to deceive, and who are only *kept from the truth because they know not where to find it*—

—D&C 123:12

Send forth the *elders of my church unto the nations* which are afar off; unto the islands of the sea; send forth unto foreign lands; call upon all nations, first upon the Gentiles, and then upon the Jews.

—D&C 133:8

And the *servants of God shall go forth,* saying with a loud voice: Fear God and give glory to him, for the hour of his judgment is come;

—D&C 133:38

Moses and Abraham on Missionary Work
(from the Pearl of Great Price)

And the Lord ordained Noah after his own order, and commanded him that he should *go forth and declare his Gospel* unto the children of men, even as it was given unto Enoch.

—Moses 8:19

And I will make of thee a great nation, and I will bless thee above measure, and make thy name great among all nations, and thou shalt be a blessing unto thy seed after thee, that *in their hands they shall bear this ministry* and Priesthood unto all nations;

—Abraham 2:9

The Prophet on Missionary Work

You are making a sacrifice, but it is not a sacrifice, because you will get more than you give up, you will gain more than you give, and it will prove to be an investment with tremendous returns, it will prove to be a blessing instead of a sacrifice. No one who ever served this work as a missionary, who gave his or her best efforts, need worry about making a sacrifice, because there will come blessings into the life of that individual for as long as he or she lives. I have not the slightest doubt about that.

—President Gordon B. Hinckley

Other Scriptures on Missionary Work

Why do we have companions?
Ecclesiastes 4:9-10

9 Two [are] better than one; because they have a good reward for their labour.

10 For if they fall, the one will lift up his fellow: but woe to him [that is] alone when he falleth; for [he hath] not another to help him up.

❧

Believers shall have the power
Mark 16:17-18

17 And these signs shall follow them that believe; In my name shall they cast out devils; they shall speak with new tongues;

18 They shall take up serpents; and if they drink any deadly thing, it shall not hurt them; they shall lay hands on the sick, and they shall recover.

❧

Wo unto me
1 Corinthians 9:16

For though I preach the gospel, I have nothing to glory of: for necessity is laid upon me; yea, woe is unto me, if I preach not the gospel!

❧

O that I were an angel
Alma 29:1-3, 6-7, 9

1 O that I were an angel, and could have the wish of mine heart, that I might go forth and speak with the trump of God, with a voice to shake the earth, and cry repentance unto every people!

2 Yea, I would declare unto every soul, as with the voice of thunder, repentance and the plan of redemption, that they should repent and come unto our God, that there might not be more sorrow upon all the face of the earth.

3 But behold, I am a man, and do sin in my wish; for I ought to be content with the things which the Lord hath allotted unto me.

6 Now, seeing that I know these things, why should I desire more than to perform the work to which I have been called?

7 Why should I desire that I were an angel, that I could speak unto all the ends of the earth?

9 I know that which the Lord hath commanded me, and I glory in it. I do not glory of myself, but I glory in that which the Lord hath commanded me; yea, and this is my glory, that perhaps I may be an instrument in the hands of God to bring some soul to repentance; and this is my joy.

❧

What to preach
Alma 37:33-35

33 Preach unto them repentance, and faith on the Lord Jesus Christ; teach them to humble themselves and to be meek and lowly in heart; teach them to withstand every temptation of the devil, with their faith on the Lord Jesus Christ.

34 Teach them to never be weary of good works, but to be meek and lowly in heart; for such shall find rest to their souls.

35 O, remember, my son, and learn wisdom in thy youth; yea, learn in thy youth to keep the commandments of God.

❧

The simple and the weak shall proclaim
D&C 1:23

That the fulness of my gospel might be proclaimed by the weak and the simple unto the ends of the world, and before kings and rulers.

❧

Whether by the voice of God or his servants
D&C 1:38

What I the Lord have spoken, I have spoken, and I excuse not myself; and though the heavens and the earth pass away, my word shall not pass away, but shall all be fulfilled, whether by mine own voice or by the voice of my servants, it is the same.

❧

Qualifications of a missionary
D&C 4:1-7

1 Now behold, a marvelous work is about to come forth among the children of men.

2 Therefore, O ye that embark in the service of God, see that ye serve him with all your heart, might, mind and strength, that ye may stand blameless before God at the last day.

3 Therefore, if ye have desires to serve God ye are called to the work;

4 For behold the field is white already to harvest; and lo, he that thrusteth in his sickle with his might, the same layeth up in store that he perisheth not, but bringeth salvation to his soul;

5 And faith, hope, charity and love, with an eye single to the glory of God, qualify him for the work.

6 Remember faith, virtue, knowledge, temperance, patience, brotherly kindness, godliness, charity, humility, diligence.

7 Ask, and ye shall receive; knock, and it shall be opened unto you. Amen.

Serve with all your heart
D&C 4:2

Therefore, O ye that embark in the service of God, see that ye serve him with all your heart, might, mind and strength, that ye may stand blameless before God at the last day.

Missionary blessed
D&C 6:29-30

29 Verily, verily, I say unto you, if they reject my words, and this part of my gospel and ministry, blessed are ye, for they can do no more unto you than unto me.

30 And even if they do unto you even as they have done unto me, blessed are ye, for you shall dwell with me in glory.

The worth of souls
D&C 18:10, 13, 15-16

10 Remember the worth of souls is great in the sight of God;

13 And how great is his joy in the soul that repenteth!

15 And if it so be that you should labor all your days in crying repentance unto this people, and bring, save it be one soul unto me, how great shall be your joy with him in the kingdom of my Father!

16 And now, if your joy will be great with one soul that you have brought unto me into the kingdom of my Father, how great will be your joy if you should bring many souls unto me!

Missionaries must be ordained
D&C 42:11

Again I say unto you, that it shall not be given to any one to go forth to preach my gospel, or to build up my church, except he be ordained by some one who has authority, and it is known to the church that he has authority and has been regularly ordained by the heads of the church.

Duties of a missionary
D&C 58:47

Let them preach by the way, and bear testimony of the truth in all places, and call upon the rich, the high and the low, and the poor to repent.

❧

The Lord is not pleased
D&C 60:2-3

2 But with some I am not well pleased, for they will not open their mouths, but they hide the talent which I have given unto them, because of the fear of man. Wo unto such, for mine anger is kindled against them.

3 And it shall come to pass, if they are not more faithful unto me, it shall be taken away, even that which they have.

❧

The gospel is the stone cut without hands
D&C 65:2

2 The keys of the kingdom of God are committed unto man on the earth, and from thence shall the gospel roll forth unto the ends of the earth, as the stone which is cut out of the mountain without hands shall roll forth, until it has filled the whole earth.

❧

Every man should warn his neighbor
D&C 88:81-82

81 Behold, I sent you out to testify and warn the people, and it becometh every man who hath been warned to warn his neighbor.

82 Therefore, they are left without excuse, and their sins are upon their own heads.

❧

Every man shall hear the fulness of the gospel
D&C 90:11

For it shall come to pass in that day, that every man shall hear the fulness of the gospel in his own tongue, and in his own language, through those who are ordained unto this power, by the administration of the Comforter, shed forth upon them for the revelation of Jesus Christ.

❧

The Eight Great Book of Mormon Missionaries:

Abinidi, the prophet, who preached to the wicked Nephite King Noah and his equally wicked priests, who burned him at the stake

Alma the Elder, one of the wicked Nephite priests of King Noah, who was converted by the testimony of Abinidi, and then became one of the great leaders and missionaries in the Book of Mormon

Alma the Younger, the rebellious son of Alma the Elder, who went around with the four sons of Mosiah causing trouble for the church, until a angel called him to repentance and then struck him dumb; also one of the great leaders and missionaries in the Book of Mormon

Amulek, one of Alma's converts, who served many missions with Alma; they were imprisoned and watched church members burned before miraculously escaping; they converted Zeezrom, who became a great missionary

Ammon, one of the converted four sons of Mosiah, who spent 14 years on a mission among the Lamanites; he offered himself as a servant to the Lamanite King Lamoni, serving as a shepherd; after Ammon's miraculous defense of the king's flocks, King Lamoni was converted, and served a mission with Ammon

Aaron, one of the converted four sons of Mosiah, who also spent 14 years on a mission among the Lamanites; he was imprisoned and later freed by Ammon and King Lamoni; he taught King Lamoni's father and court

Nephi and Lehi, the sons of Helaman, who were named after the original Nephi and Lehi, who devoted the remainder of their lives to missionary work among both the Nephites and Lamanites; they were imprisoned, then encircled by fire as they taught, before miraculously escaping; they baptized many Lamanites

Samuel the Lamanite, a converted Lamanite who called the then wicked Nephites to repentance from the wall surrounding their city, referring them to the above Nephi for baptism; the wicked Nephites tried to kill Samuel with stones and arrows, but could not hit him

Following are their stories, pieced together from the scriptures, with added notes, for ease and pleasure in reading.

᙮

The Mission of Abinadi

The first discussion
Mosiah 11

20 And it came to pass that there was a man among them whose name was Abinadi; and he went forth among them, and began to prophesy, saying: Behold, thus saith the Lord, and thus hath he commanded me, saying, Go forth, and say unto this people, thus saith the Lord—Wo be unto this people, for I have seen their abominations, and their wickedness, and their whoredoms; and except they repent I will visit them in mine anger.

21 And except they repent and turn to the Lord their God, behold, I will deliver them into the hands of their enemies; yea, and they shall be brought into bondage; and they shall be afflicted by the hand of their enemies.

22 And it shall come to pass that they shall know that I am the Lord their God, and am a jealous God, visiting the iniquities of my people.

23 And it shall come to pass that except this people repent and turn unto the Lord their God, they shall be brought into bondage; and none shall deliver them, except it be the Lord the Almighty God.

24 Yea, and it shall come to pass that when they shall cry unto me I will be slow to hear their cries; yea, and I will suffer them that they be smitten by their enemies.

25 And except they repent in sackcloth and ashes, and cry mightily to the Lord their God, I will not hear their prayers, neither will I deliver them out of their afflictions; and thus saith the Lord, and thus hath he commanded me.

The escape

26 Now it came to pass that when Abinadi had spoken these words unto them they were wroth with him, and sought to take away his life; but the Lord delivered him out of their hands.

The warrant

27 Now when king Noah had heard of the words which Abinadi had spoken unto the people, he was also wroth; and he said: Who is Abinadi, that I and my people should be judged of him, or who is the Lord, that shall bring upon my people such great affliction?

28 I command you to bring Abinadi hither, that I may slay him, for he has said these things that he might stir up my people to anger one with another, and to raise contentions among my people; therefore I will slay him.

29 Now the eyes of the people were blinded; therefore they hardened their hearts against the words of Abinadi, and they sought from that time forward to take him. And king Noah hardened his heart against the word of the Lord, and he did not repent of his evil doings.

The second discussion
Mosiah 12

1 And it came to pass that after the space of two years that Abinadi came among them in disguise, that they knew him not, and began to prophesy among them, saying: Thus has the Lord commanded me, saying— Abinadi, go and prophesy unto this my people, for they have hardened their hearts against my words; they have repented not of their evil doings; therefore, I will visit them in my anger, yea, in my fierce anger will I visit them in their iniquities and abominations.

2 Yea, wo be unto this generation! And the Lord said unto me: Stretch forth thy hand and prophesy saying: Thus saith the Lord, it shall come to pass that this generation, because of their iniquities, shall be brought into bondage, and shall be smitten on the cheek; yea, and shall be driven by men, and shall be slain; and the vultures of the air, and the dogs, yea, and the wild beasts, shall devour their flesh.

3 And it shall come to pass that the life of king Noah shall be valued even as a garment in a hot furnace; for he shall know that I am the Lord.

4 And it shall come to pass that I will smite this my people with sore afflictions, yea, with famine and with pestilence; and I will cause that they shall howl all the day long.

5 Yea, and I will cause that they shall have burdens lashed upon their backs; and they shall be driven before like a dumb ass.

6 And it shall come to pass that I will send forth hail among them, and it shall smite them; and they shall also be smitten with the east wind; and insects shall pester their land also, and devour their grain.

7 And they shall be smitten with a great pestilence—and all this will I do because of their iniquities and abominations.

8 And it shall come to pass that except they repent I will utterly destroy them from off the face of the earth; yet they shall leave a record behind them, and I will preserve them for other nations which shall possess the land; yea, even this will I do that I may discover the abominations of this people to other nations. And many things did Abinadi prophesy against this people.

The capture and prosecution

9 And it came to pass that they were angry with him; and they took him and carried him bound before the king, and said unto the king: Behold, we have brought a man before thee who has prophesied evil concerning thy people, and saith that God will destroy them.

10 And he also prophesieth evil concerning thy life, and saith that thy life shall be as a garment in a furnace of fire.

11 And again, he saith that thou shalt be as a stalk, even as a dry stalk of the field, which is run over by the beasts and trodden under foot.

12 And again, he saith thou shalt be as the blossoms of a thistle, which, when it is fully ripe, if the wind bloweth, it is driven forth upon the face of the land. And he pretendeth the Lord hath spoken it. And he saith all this shall come upon thee except thou repent, and this because of thine iniquities.

13 And now, O king, what great evil hast thou done, or what great sins have thy people committed, that we should be condemned of God or judged of this man?

14 And now, O king, behold, we are guiltless, and thou, O king, hast not sinned; therefore, this man has lied concerning you, and he has prophesied in vain.

15 And behold, we are strong, we shall not come into bondage, or be taken captive by our enemies; yea, and thou hast prospered in the land, and thou shalt also prosper.

16 Behold, here is the man, we deliver him into thy hands; thou mayest do with him as seemeth thee good.

The imprisonment

17 And it came to pass that king Noah caused that Abinadi should be cast into prison; and he commanded that the priests should gather themselves together that he might hold a council with them what he should do with him.

The trial

18 And it came to pass that they said unto the king: Bring him hither that we may question him; and the king commanded that he should be brought before them.

19 And they began to question him, that they might cross him, that thereby they might have wherewith to accuse him; but he answered them boldly, and withstood all their questions, yea, to their astonishment; for he did withstand them in all their questions, and did confound them in all their words.

20 And it came to pass that one of them said unto him: What meaneth the words which are written, and which have been taught by our fathers, saying:

21 How beautiful upon the mountains are the feet of him that bringeth good tidings; that publisheth peace; that bringeth good tidings of good; that publisheth salvation; that saith unto Zion, Thy God reigneth;

22 Thy watchmen shall lift up the voice; with the voice together shall they sing; for they shall see eye to eye when the Lord shall bring again Zion;

23 Break forth into joy; sing together ye waste places of Jerusalem; for the Lord hath comforted his people, he hath redeemed Jerusalem;

24 The Lord hath made bare his holy arm in the eyes of all the nations, and all the ends of the earth shall see the salvation of our God?

The third discussion

25 And now Abinadi said unto them: Are you priests, and pretend to teach this people, and to understand the spirit of prophesying, and yet desire to know of me what these things mean?

26 I say unto you, wo be unto you for perverting the ways of the Lord! For if ye understand these things ye have not taught them; therefore, ye have perverted the ways of the Lord.

27 Ye have not applied your hearts to understanding; therefore, ye have not been wise. Therefore, what teach ye this people?

28 And they said: We teach the law of Moses.

29 And again he said unto them: If ye teach the law of Moses why do ye not keep it? Why do ye set your hearts upon riches? Why do ye commit whoredoms and spend your strength with harlots, yea, and cause this people to commit sin, that the Lord has cause to send me to prophesy against this people, yea, even a great evil against this people?

30 Know ye not that I speak the truth? Yea, ye know that I speak the truth; and you ought to tremble before God.

31 And it shall come to pass that ye shall be smitten for your iniquities, for ye have said that ye teach the law of Moses. And what know ye concerning the law of Moses? Doth salvation come by the law of Moses? What say ye?

32 And they answered and said that salvation did come by the law of Moses.

33 But now Abinadi said unto them: I know if ye keep the commandments of God ye shall be saved; yea, if ye keep the commandments which the Lord delivered unto Moses in the mount of Sinai, saying:

The fourth discussion—The Ten Commandments

34 I am the Lord thy God, who hath brought thee out of the land of Egypt, out of the house of bondage.

35 Thou shalt have no other God before me.

36 Thou shalt not make unto thee any graven image, or any likeness of any thing in heaven above, or things which are in the earth beneath.

37 Now Abinadi said unto them, Have ye done all this? I say unto you, Nay, ye have not. And have ye taught this people that they should do all these things? I say unto you, Nay, ye have not.

The seizure and deliverance
Mosiah 13

1 And now when the king had heard these words, he said unto his priests: Away with this fellow, and slay him; for what have we to do with him, for he is mad.

2 And they stood forth and attempted to lay their hands on him; but he withstood them, and said unto them:

3 Touch me not, for God shall smite you if ye lay your hands upon me, for I have not delivered the message which the Lord sent me to deliver; neither have I told you that which ye requested that I should tell; therefore, God will not suffer that I shall be destroyed at this time.

4 But I must fulfil the commandments wherewith God has commanded me; and because I have told you the truth ye are angry with me. And again, because I have spoken the word of God ye have judged me that I am mad.

5 Now it came to pass after Abinadi had spoken these words that the people of king Noah durst not lay their hands on him, for the Spirit of the Lord was upon him; and his face shone with exceeding luster, even as Moses' did while in the mount of Sinai, while speaking with the Lord.

The fifth discussion

6 And he spake with power and authority from God; and he continued his words, saying:

7 Ye see that ye have not power to slay me, therefore I finish my message. Yea, and I perceive that it cuts you to your hearts because I tell you the truth concerning your iniquities.

8 Yea, and my words fill you with wonder and amazement, and with anger.

9 But I finish my message; and then it matters not whither I go, if it so be that I am saved.

10 But this much I tell you, what you do with me, after this, shall be as a type and a shadow of things which are to come.

11 And now I read unto you the remainder of the commandments of God, for I perceive that they are not written in your hearts; I perceive that ye have studied and taught iniquity the most part of your lives.

The Ten Commandments continued

12 And now, ye remember that I said unto you: Thou shalt not make unto thee any graven image, or any likeness of things which are in heaven above, or which are in the earth beneath, or which are in the water under the earth.

13 And again: Thou shalt not bow down thyself unto them, nor serve them; for I the Lord thy God am a jealous God, visiting the iniquities of the fathers upon the children, unto the third and fourth generations of them that hate me;

14 And showing mercy unto thousands of them that love me and keep my commandments.

15 Thou shalt not take the name of the Lord thy God in vain; for the Lord will not hold him guiltless that taketh his name in vain.

16 Remember the sabbath day, to keep it holy.

17 Six days shalt thou labor, and do all thy work;

18 But the seventh day, the sabbath of the Lord thy God, thou shalt not do any work, thou, nor thy son, nor thy daughter, thy man-servant, nor thy maid-servant, nor thy cattle, nor thy stranger that is within thy gates;

19 For in six days the Lord made heaven and earth, and the sea, and all that in them is; wherefore the Lord blessed the sabbath day, and hallowed it.

20 Honor thy father and thy mother, that thy days may be long upon the land which the Lord thy God giveth thee.

21 Thou shalt not kill.

22 Thou shalt not commit adultery. Thou shalt not steal.

23 Thou shalt not bear false witness against thy neighbor.

24 Thou shalt not covet thy neighbor's house, thou shalt not covet thy neighbor's wife, nor his man-servant, nor his maid-servant, nor his ox, nor his ass, nor anything that is thy neighbor's.

25 And it came to pass that after Abinadi had made an end of these sayings that he said unto them: Have ye taught this people that they should observe to do all these things for to keep these commandments?

26 I say unto you, Nay; for if ye had, the Lord would not have caused me to come forth and to prophesy evil concerning this people.

The sixth discussion—the law of Moses

27 And now ye have said that salvation cometh by the law of Moses. I say unto you that it is expedient that ye should keep the law of Moses as yet; but I say unto you, that the time shall come when it shall no more be expedient to keep the law of Moses.

28 And moreover, I say unto you, that salvation doth not come by the law alone; and were it not for the atonement, which God himself shall make for the sins and iniquities of his people, that they must unavoidably perish, notwithstanding the law of Moses.

29 And now I say unto you that it was expedient that there should be a law given to the children of Israel, yea, even a very strict law; for they were a stiffnecked people, quick to do iniquity, and slow to remember the Lord their God;

30 Therefore there was a law given them, yea, a law of performances and of ordinances, a law which they were to observe strictly from day to day, to keep them in remembrance of God and their duty towards him.

31 But behold, I say unto you, that all these things were types of things to come.

32 And now, did they understand the law? I say unto you, Nay, they did not all understand the law; and this because of the hardness of their hearts; for they understood not that there could not any man be saved except it were through the redemption of God.

The seventh discussion—the Messiah

33 For behold, did not Moses prophesy unto them concerning the coming of the Messiah, and that God should redeem his people? Yea, and even all the prophets who have prophesied ever since the world began— have they not spoken more or less concerning these things?

34 Have they not said that God himself should come down among the children of men, and take upon him the form of a man, and go forth in mighty power upon the face of the earth?

35 Yea, and have they not said also that he should bring to pass the resurrection of the dead, and that he, himself, should be oppressed and afflicted?

Mosiah 14

1 Yea, even doth not Isaiah say: Who hath believed our report, and to whom is the arm of the Lord revealed?

2 For he shall grow up before him as a tender plant, and as a root out of dry ground; he hath no form nor comeliness; and when we shall see him there is no beauty that we should desire him.

3 He is despised and rejected of men; a man of sorrows, and acquainted with grief; and we hid as it were our faces from him; he was despised, and we esteemed him not.

4 Surely he has borne our griefs, and carried our sorrows; yet we did esteem him stricken, smitten of God, and afflicted.

5 But he was wounded for our transgressions, he was bruised for our iniquities; the chastisement of our peace was upon him; and with his stripes we are healed.

6 All we, like sheep, have gone astray; we have turned every one to his own way; and the Lord hath laid on him the iniquities of us all.

7 He was oppressed, and he was afflicted, yet he opened not his mouth; he is brought as a lamb to the slaughter, and as a sheep before her shearers is dumb so he opened not his mouth.

8 He was taken from prison and from judgment; and who shall declare his generation? For he was cut off out of the land of the living; for the transgressions of my people was he stricken.

9 And he made his grave with the wicked, and with the rich in his death; because he had done no evil, neither was any deceit in his mouth.

10 Yet it pleased the Lord to bruise him; he hath put him to grief; when thou shalt make his soul an offering for sin he shall see his seed, he shall prolong his days, and the pleasure of the Lord shall prosper in his hand.

11 He shall see the travail of his soul, and shall be satisfied; by his knowledge shall my righteous servant justify many; for he shall bear their iniquities.

12 Therefore will I divide him a portion with the great, and he shall divide the spoil with the strong; because he hath poured out his soul unto death; and he was numbered with the transgressors; and he bore the sins of many, and made intercession for the transgressors.

Mosiah 15

1 And now Abinadi said unto them: I would that ye should understand that God himself shall come down among the children of men, and shall redeem his people.

2 And because he dwelleth in flesh he shall be called the Son of God, and having subjected the flesh to the will of the Father, being the Father and the Son—

3 The Father, because he was conceived by the power of God; and the Son, because of the flesh; thus becoming the Father and Son—

4 And they are one God, yea, the very Eternal Father of heaven and of earth.

5 And thus the flesh becoming subject to the Spirit, or the Son to the Father, being one God, suffereth temptation, and yieldeth not to the temptation, but suffereth himself to be mocked, and scourged, and cast out, and disowned by his people.

6 And after all this, after working many mighty miracles among the children of men, he shall be led, yea, even as Isaiah said, as a sheep before the shearer is dumb, so he opened not his mouth.

7 Yea, even so he shall be led, crucified, and slain, the flesh becoming subject even unto death, the will of the Son being swallowed up in the will of the Father.

8 And thus God breaketh the bands of death, having gained the victory over death; giving the Son power to make intercession for the children of men—

9 Having ascended into heaven, having the bowels of mercy; being filled with compassion towards the children of men; standing betwixt them and justice; having broken the bands of death, taken upon himself their iniquity and their transgressions, having redeemed them, and satisfied the demands of justice.

The eighth discussion—the prophets

10 And now I say unto you, who shall declare his generation? Behold, I say unto you, that when his soul has been made an offering for sin he shall see his seed. And now what say ye? And who shall be his seed?

11 Behold I say unto you, that whosoever has heard the words of the prophets, yea, all the holy prophets who have prophesied concerning the coming of the Lord—I say unto you, that all those who have hearkened unto their words, and believed that the Lord would redeem his people, and have looked forward to that day for a remission of their sins, I say unto you, that these are his seed, or they are the heirs of the kingdom of God.

12 For these are they whose sins he has borne; these are they for whom he has died, to redeem them from their transgressions. And now, are they not his seed?

13 Yea, and are not the prophets, every one that has opened his mouth to prophesy, that has not fallen into transgression, I mean all the holy prophets ever since the world began? I say unto you that they are his seed.

14 And these are they who have published peace, who have brought good tidings of good, who have published salvation; and said unto Zion: Thy God reigneth!

15 And O how beautiful upon the mountains were their feet!

16 And again, how beautiful upon the mountains are the feet of those that are still publishing peace!

17 And again, how beautiful upon the mountains are the feet of those who shall hereafter publish peace, yea, from this time henceforth and forever!

18 And behold, I say unto you, this is not all. For O how beautiful upon the mountains are the feet of him that bringeth good tidings, that is the founder of peace, yea, even the Lord, who has redeemed his people; yea, him who has granted salvation unto his people;

19 For were it not for the redemption which he hath made for his people, which was prepared from the foundation of the world, I say unto you, were it not for this, all mankind must have perished.

The ninth discussion—the resurrection

20 But behold, the bands of death shall be broken, and the Son reigneth, and hath power over the dead; therefore, he bringeth to pass the resurrection of the dead.

21 And there cometh a resurrection, even a first resurrection; yea, even a resurrection of those that have been, and who are, and who shall be, even until the resurrection of Christ—for so shall he be called.

22 And now, the resurrection of all the prophets, and all those that have believed in their words, or all those that have kept the commandments of God, shall come forth in the first resurrection; therefore, they are the first resurrection.

23 They are raised to dwell with God who has redeemed them; thus they have eternal life through Christ, who has broken the bands of death.

24 And these are those who have part in the first resurrection; and these are they that have died before Christ came, in their ignorance, not having salvation declared unto them. And thus the Lord bringeth about the restoration of these; and they have a part in the first resurrection, or have eternal life, being redeemed by the Lord.

25 And little children also have eternal life.

The fear and trembling

26 But behold, and fear, and tremble before God, for ye ought to tremble; for the Lord redeemeth none such that rebel against him and die in their sins; yea, even all those that have perished in their sins ever since the world began, that have wilfully rebelled against God, that have known the commandments of God, and would not keep them; these are they that have no part in the first resurrection.

27 Therefore ought ye not to tremble? For salvation cometh to none such; for the Lord hath redeemed none such; yea, neither can the Lord redeem such; for he cannot deny himself; for he cannot deny justice when it has its claim.

28 And now I say unto you that the time shall come that the salvation of the Lord shall be declared to every nation, kindred, tongue, and people.

29 Yea, Lord, thy watchmen shall lift up their voice; with the voice together shall they sing; for they shall see eye to eye, when the Lord shall bring again Zion.

30 Break forth into joy, sing together, ye waste places of Jerusalem; for the Lord hath comforted his people, he hath redeemed Jerusalem.

31 The Lord hath made bare his holy arm in the eyes of all the nations; and all the ends of the earth shall see the salvation of our God.

Mosiah 16

1 And now, it came to pass that after Abinadi had spoken these words he stretched forth his hand and said: The time shall come when all shall see the salvation of the Lord; when every nation, kindred, tongue, and people shall see eye to eye and shall confess before God that his judgments are just.

2 And then shall the wicked be cast out, and they shall have cause to howl, and weep, and wail, and gnash their teeth; and this because they would not hearken unto the voice of the Lord; therefore the Lord redeemeth them not.

3 For they are carnal and devilish, and the devil has power over them; yea, even that old serpent that did beguile our first parents, which was the cause of their fall; which was the cause of all mankind becoming carnal, sensual, devilish, knowing evil from good, subjecting themselves to the devil.

4 Thus all mankind were lost; and behold, they would have been endlessly lost were it not that God redeemed his people from their lost and fallen state.

5 But remember that he that persists in his own carnal nature, and goes on in the ways of sin and rebellion against God, remaineth in his fallen state and the devil hath all power over him. Therefore, he is as though there was no redemption made, being an enemy to God; and also is the devil an enemy to God.

6 And now if Christ had not come into the world, speaking of things to come as though they had already come, there could have been no redemption.

The resurrection continued

7 And if Christ had not risen from the dead, or have broken the bands of death that the grave should have no victory, and that death should have no sting, there could have been no resurrection.

8 But there is a resurrection, therefore the grave hath no victory, and the sting of death is swallowed up in Christ.

9 He is the light and the life of the world; yea, a light that is endless, that can never be darkened; yea, and also a life which is endless, that there can be no more death.

10 Even this mortal shall put on immortality, and this corruption shall put on incorruption, and shall be brought to stand before the bar of God, to be judged of him according to their works whether they be good or whether they be evil—

11 If they be good, to the resurrection of endless life and happiness; and if they be evil, to the resurrection of endless damnation, being delivered up to the devil, who hath subjected them, which is damnation—

12 Having gone according to their own carnal wills and desires; having never called upon the Lord while the arms of mercy were extended towards them; for the arms of mercy were extended towards them, and they would not; they being warned of their iniquities and yet they would not depart from them; and they were commanded to repent and yet they would not repent.

13 And now, ought ye not to tremble and repent of your sins, and remember that only in and through Christ ye can be saved?

14 Therefore, if ye teach the law of Moses, also teach that it is a shadow of those things which are to come—

15 Teach them that redemption cometh through Christ the Lord, who is the very Eternal Father. Amen.

The verdict
Mosiah 17

1 And now it came to pass that when Abinadi had finished these sayings, that the king commanded that the priests should take him and cause that he should be put to death.

The conversion and escape of Alma

2 But there was one among them whose name was Alma, he also being a descendant of Nephi. And he was a young man, and he believed the words which Abinadi had spoken, for he knew concerning the iniquity which Abinadi had testified against them; therefore he began to plead with the king that he would not be angry with Abinadi, but suffer that he might depart in peace.

3 But the king was more wroth, and caused that Alma should be cast out from among them, and sent his servants after him that they might slay him.

4 But he fled from before them and hid himself that they found him not. And he being concealed for many days did write all the words which Abinadi had spoken.

The second imprisonment
5 And it came to pass that the king caused that his guards should surround Abinadi and take him; and they bound him and cast him into prison.

The trial

6 And after three days, having counseled with his priests, he caused that he should again be brought before him.

7 And he said unto him: Abinadi, we have found an accusation against thee, and thou art worthy of death.

8 For thou hast said that God himself should come down among the children of men; and now, for this cause thou shalt be put to death unless thou wilt recall all the words which thou hast spoken evil concerning me and my people.

The defense

9 Now Abinadi said unto him: I say unto you, I will not recall the words which I have spoken unto you concerning this people, for they are true; and that ye may know of their surety I have suffered myself that I have fallen into your hands.

10 Yea, and I will suffer even until death, and I will not recall my words, and they shall stand as a testimony against you. And if ye slay me ye will shed innocent blood, and this shall also stand as a testimony against you at the last day.

The near acquittal

11 And now king Noah was about to release him, for he feared his word; for he feared that the judgments of God would come upon him.

The mob

12 But the priests lifted up their voices against him, and began to accuse him, saying: He has reviled the king. Therefore the king was stirred up in anger against him, and he delivered him up that he might be slain.

The martyrdom

13 And it came to pass that they took him and bound him, and scourged his skin with faggots, yea, even unto death.

14 And now when the flames began to scorch him, he cried unto them, saying:

The final prophesy

15 Behold, even as ye have done unto me, so shall it come to pass that thy seed shall cause that many shall suffer the pains that I do suffer, even the pains of death by fire; and this because they believe in the salvation of the Lord their God.

16 And it will come to pass that ye shall be afflicted with all manner of diseases because of your iniquities.

17 Yea, and ye shall be smitten on every hand, and shall be driven and scattered to and fro, even as a wild flock is driven by wild and ferocious beasts.

18 And in that day ye shall be hunted, and ye shall be taken by the hand of your enemies, and then ye shall suffer, as I suffer, the pains of death by fire.

19 Thus God executeth vengeance upon those that destroy his people. O God, receive my soul.

The end

20 And now, when Abinadi had said these words, he fell, having suffered death by fire; yea, having been put to death because he would not deny the commandments of God, having sealed the truth of his words by his death.

The Conversion and Mission of Alma the Elder

The conversion and escape of Alma
Mosiah 17

2 But there was one among them whose name was Alma, he also being a descendant of Nephi. And he was a young man, and he believed the words which Abinadi had spoken, for he knew concerning the iniquity which Abinadi had testified against them; therefore he began to plead with the king that he would not be angry with Abinadi, but suffer that he might depart in peace.

3 But the king was more wroth, and caused that Alma should be cast out from among them, and sent his servants after him that they might slay him.

4 But he fled from before them and hid himself that they found him not. And he being concealed for many days did write all the words which Abinadi had spoken.

Alma begins teaching
Mosiah 18

1 And now, it came to pass that Alma, who had fled from the servants of king Noah, repented of his sins and iniquities, and went about privately among the people, and began to teach the words of Abinadi—

2 Yea, concerning that which was to come, and also concerning the resurrection of the dead, and the redemption of the people, which was to be brought to pass through the power, and sufferings, and death of Christ, and his resurrection and ascension into heaven.

3 And as many as would hear his word he did teach. And he taught them privately, that it might not come to the knowledge of the king. And many did believe his words.

The Waters of Mormon

4 And it came to pass that as many as did believe him did go forth to a place which was called Mormon, having received its name from the king, being in the borders of the land having been infested, by times or at seasons, by wild beasts.

5 Now, there was in Mormon a fountain of pure water, and Alma resorted thither, there being near the water a thicket of small trees, where he did hide himself in the daytime from the searches of the king.

6 And it came to pass that as many as believed him went thither to hear his words.

7 And it came to pass after many days there were a goodly number gathered together at the place of Mormon, to hear the words of Alma. Yea, all were gathered together that believed on his word, to hear him. And he did teach them, and did preach unto them repentance, and redemption, and faith on the Lord.

As ye are desirous

8 And it came to pass that he said unto them: Behold, here are the waters of Mormon (for thus were they called) and now, as ye are desirous to come into the fold of God, and to be called his people, and are willing to bear one another's burdens, that they may be light;

9 Yea, and are willing to mourn with those that mourn; yea, and comfort those that stand in need of comfort, and to stand as witnesses of God at all times and in all things, and in all places that ye may be in, even until death, that ye may be redeemed of God, and be numbered with those of the first resurrection, that ye may have eternal life—

10 Now I say unto you, if this be the desire of your hearts, what have you against being baptized in the name of the Lord, as a witness before him that ye have entered into a covenant with him, that ye will serve him and keep his commandments, that he may pour out his Spirit more abundantly upon you?

They clapped their hands for joy

11 And now when the people had heard these words, they clapped their hands for joy, and exclaimed: This is the desire of our hearts.

The baptisms

12 And now it came to pass that Alma took Helam, he being one of the first, and went and stood forth in the water, and cried, saying: O Lord, pour out thy Spirit upon thy servant, that he may do this work with holiness of heart.

13 And when he had said these words, the Spirit of the Lord was upon him, and he said: Helam, I baptize thee, having authority from the Almighty God, as a testimony that ye have entered into a covenant to serve him until you are dead as to the mortal body; and may the Spirit of the Lord be poured out upon you; and may he grant unto you eternal life, through the redemption of Christ, whom he has prepared from the foundation of the world.

14 And after Alma had said these words, both Alma and Helam were buried in the water; and they arose and came forth out of the water rejoicing, being filled with the Spirit.

15 And again, Alma took another, and went forth a second time into the water, and baptized him according to the first, only he did not bury himself again in the water.

16 And after this manner he did baptize every one that went forth to the place of Mormon; and they were in number about two hundred and four souls; yea, and they were baptized in the waters of Mormon, and were filled with the grace of God.

The church

17 And they were called the church of God, or the church of Christ, from that time forward. And it came to pass that whosoever was baptized by the power and authority of God was added to his church.

The ordinations

18 And it came to pass that Alma, having authority from God, ordained priests; even one priest to every fifty of their number did he ordain to preach unto them, and to teach them concerning the things pertaining to the kingdom of God.

The teaching

19 And he commanded them that they should teach nothing save it were the things which he had taught, and which had been spoken by the mouth of the holy prophets.

20 Yea, even he commanded them that they should preach nothing save it were repentance and faith on the Lord, who had redeemed his people.

No contention

21 And he commanded them that there should be no contention one with another, but that they should look forward with one eye, having one faith and one baptism, having their hearts knit together in unity and in love one towards another.

22 And thus he commanded them to preach. And thus they became the children of God.

Observe the Sabbath

23 And he commanded them that they should observe the sabbath day, and keep it holy, and also every day they should give thanks to the Lord their God.

Labor with their own hands

24 And he also commanded them that the priests whom he had ordained should labor with their own hands for their support.

25 And there was one day in every week that was set apart that they should gather themselves together to teach the people, and to worship the Lord their God, and also, as often as it was in their power, to assemble themselves together.

26 And the priests were not to depend upon the people for their support; but for their labor they were to receive the grace of God, that they might wax strong in the Spirit, having the knowledge of God, that they might teach with power and authority from God.

Impart of their substance

27 And again Alma commanded that the people of the church should impart of their substance, every one according to that which he had; if he have more abundantly he should impart more abundantly; and of him that had but little, but little should be required; and to him that had not should be given.

28 And thus they should impart of their substance of their own free will and good desires towards God, and to those priests that stood in need, yea, and to every needy, naked soul.

29 And this he said unto them, having been commanded of God; and they did walk uprightly before God, imparting to one another both temporally and spiritually according to their needs and their wants.

30 And now it came to pass that all this was done in Mormon, yea, by the waters of Mormon, in the forest that was near the waters of Mormon; yea, the place of Mormon, the waters of Mormon, the forest of Mormon, how beautiful are they to the eyes of them who there came to the knowledge of their Redeemer; yea, and how blessed are they, for they shall sing to his praise forever.

31 And these things were done in the borders of the land, that they might not come to the knowledge of the king.

The warrant

32 But behold, it came to pass that the king, having discovered a movement among the people, sent his servants to watch them. Therefore on the day that they were assembling themselves together to hear the word of the Lord they were discovered unto the king.

33 And now the king said that Alma was stirring up the people to rebellion against him; therefore he sent his army to destroy them.

The escape

34 And it came to pass that Alma and the people of the Lord were apprised of the coming of the king's army; therefore they took their tents and their families and departed into the wilderness.

35 And they were in number about four hundred and fifty souls.

The Conversion and Mission of Alma the Younger

The rebellion
Mosiah 27

8 Now the sons of Mosiah were numbered among the unbelievers; and also one of the sons of Alma was numbered among them, he being called Alma, after his father; nevertheless, he became a very wicked and an idolatrous man. And he was a man of many words, and did speak much flattery to the people; therefore he led many of the people to do after the manner of his iniquities.

9 And he became a great hinderment to the prosperity of the church of God; stealing away the hearts of the people; causing much dissension among the people; giving a chance for the enemy of God to exercise his power over them.

10 And now it came to pass that while he was going about to destroy the church of God, for he did go about secretly with the sons of Mosiah seeking to destroy the church, and to lead astray the people of the Lord, contrary to the commandments of God, or even the king—

The angel

11 And as I said unto you, as they were going about rebelling against God, behold, the angel of the Lord appeared unto them; and he descended as it were in a cloud; and he spake as it were with a voice of thunder, which caused the earth to shake upon which they stood;

12 And so great was their astonishment, that they fell to the earth, and understood not the words which he spake unto them.

13 Nevertheless he cried again, saying: Alma, arise and stand forth, for why persecutest thou the church of God? For the Lord hath said: This is my church, and I will establish it; and nothing shall overthrow it, save it is the transgression of my people.

14 And again, the angel said: Behold, the Lord hath heard the prayers of his people, and also the prayers of his servant, Alma, who is thy father; for he has prayed with much faith concerning thee that thou mightest be brought to the knowledge of the truth; therefore, for this purpose have I come to convince thee of the power and authority of God, that the prayers of his servants might be answered according to their faith.

15 And now behold, can ye dispute the power of God? For behold, doth not my voice shake the earth? And can ye not also behold me before you? And I am sent from God.

16 Now I say unto thee: Go, and remember the captivity of thy fathers in the land of Helam, and in the land of Nephi; and remember how great things he has done for them; for they were in bondage, and he has delivered them. And now I say unto thee, Alma, go thy way, and seek to destroy the church no more, that their prayers may be answered, and this even if thou wilt of thyself be cast off.

17 And now it came to pass that these were the last words which the angel spake unto Alma, and he departed.

The repentance

18 And now Alma and those that were with him fell again to the earth, for great was their astonishment; for with their own eyes they had beheld an angel of the Lord; and his voice was as thunder, which shook the earth; and they knew that there was nothing save the power of God that could shake the earth and cause it to tremble as though it would part asunder.

19 And now the astonishment of Alma was so great that he became dumb, that he could not open his mouth; yea, and he became weak, even that he could not move his hands; therefore he was taken by those that were with him, and carried helpless, even until he was laid before his father.

The fast and prayer

20 And they rehearsed unto his father all that had happened unto them; and his father rejoiced, for he knew that it was the power of God.

21 And he caused that a multitude should be gathered together that they might witness what the Lord had done for his son, and also for those that were with him.

22 And he caused that the priests should assemble themselves together; and they began to fast, and to pray to the Lord their God that he would open the mouth of Alma, that he might speak, and also that his limbs might receive their strength—that the eyes of the people might be opened to see and know of the goodness and glory of God.

The testimony

23 And it came to pass after they had fasted and prayed for the space of two days and two nights, the l imbs of Alma received their strength, and he stood up and began to speak unto them, bidding them to be of good comfort:

24 For, said he, I have repented of my sins, and have been redeemed of the Lord; behold I am born of the Spirit.

25 And the Lord said unto me: Marvel not that all mankind, yea, men and women, all nations, kindreds, tongues and people, must be born again; yea, born of God, changed from their carnal and fallen state, to a state of righteousness, being redeemed of God, becoming his sons and daughters;

26 And thus they become new creatures; and unless they do this, they can in nowise inherit the kingdom of God.

27 I say unto you, unless this be the case, they must be cast off; and this I know, because I was like to be cast off.

28 Nevertheless, after wading through much tribulation, repenting nigh unto death, the Lord in mercy hath seen fit to snatch me out of an everlasting burning, and I am born of God.

29 My soul hath been redeemed from the gall of bitterness and bonds of iniquity. I was in the darkest abyss; but now I behold the marvelous light of God. My soul was racked with eternal torment; but I am snatched, and my soul is pained no more.

30 I rejected my Redeemer, and denied that which had been spoken of by our fathers; but now that they may foresee that he will come, and that he remembereth every creature of his creating, he will make himself manifest unto all.

31 Yea, every knee shall bow, and every tongue confess before him. Yea, even at the last day, when all men shall stand to be judged of him, then shall they confess that he is God; then shall they confess, who live without God in the world, that the judgment of an everlasting punishment is just upon them; and they shall quake, and tremble, and shrink beneath the glance of his all-searching eye.

The mission

32 And now it came to pass that Alma began from this time forward to teach the people, and those who were with Alma at the time the angel appeared unto them, traveling round about through all the land, publishing to all the people the things which they had heard and seen, and preaching the word of God in much tribulation, being greatly persecuted by those who were unbelievers, being smitten by many of them.

33 But notwithstanding all this, they did impart much consolation to the church, confirming their faith, and exhorting them with long-suffering and much travail to keep the commandments of God.

34 And four of them were the sons of Mosiah; and their names were Ammon, and Aaron, and Omner, and Himni; these were the names of the sons of Mosiah.

35 And they traveled throughout all the land of Zarahemla, and among all the people who were under the reign of king Mosiah, zealously striving to repair all the injuries which they had done to the church, confessing all their sins, and publishing all the things which they had seen, and explaining the prophecies and the scriptures to all who desired to hear them.

36 And thus they were instruments in the hands of God in bringing many to the knowledge of the truth, yea, to the knowledge of their Redeemer.

37 And how blessed are they! For they did publish peace; they did publish good tidings of good; and they did declare unto the people that the Lord reigneth.

The Conversion and Mission of Amulek

Alma preaches in Ammonihah
Alma 8

8 And it came to pass that when Alma had come to the city of Ammonihah he began to preach the word of God unto them.

9 Now Satan had gotten great hold upon the hearts of the people of the city of Ammonihah; therefore they would not hearken unto the words of Alma.

10 Nevertheless Alma labored much in the spirit, wrestling with God in mighty prayer, that he would pour out his Spirit upon the people who were in the city; that he would also grant that he might baptize them unto repentance.

The people reject him

11 Nevertheless, they hardened their hearts, saying unto him: Behold, we know that thou art Alma; and we know that thou art high priest over the church which thou hast established in many parts of the land, according to your tradition; and we are not of thy church, and we do not believe in such foolish traditions.

12 And now we know that because we are not of thy church we know that thou hast no power over us; and thou hast delivered up the judgment-seat unto Nephihah; therefore thou art not the chief judge over us.

Alma departs

13 Now when the people had said this, and withstood all his words, and reviled him, and spit upon him, and caused that he should be cast out of their city, he departed thence and took his journey towards the city which was called Aaron.

An angel commands Alma to return

14 And it came to pass that while he was journeying thither, being weighed down with sorrow, wading through much tribulation and anguish of soul, because of the wickedness of the people who were in the city of Ammonihah, it came to pass while Alma was thus weighed down with sorrow, behold an angel of the Lord appeared unto him, saying:

15 Blessed art thou, Alma; therefore, lift up thy head and rejoice, for thou hast great cause to rejoice; for thou hast been faithful in keeping the commandments of God from the time which thou receivedst thy first message from him. Behold, I am he that delivered it unto you.

16 And behold, I am sent to command thee that thou return to the city of Ammonihah, and preach again unto the people of the city; yea, preach unto them. Yea, say unto them, except they repent the Lord God will destroy them.

17 For behold, they do study at this time that they may destroy the liberty of thy people, (for thus saith the Lord) which is contrary to the statutes, and judgments, and commandments which he has given unto his people.

Alma returns

18 Now it came to pass that after Alma had received his message from the angel of the Lord he returned speedily to the land of Ammonihah. And he entered the city by another way, yea, by the way which is on the south of the city of Ammonihah.

Alma fed by Amulek

19 And as he entered the city he was an hungered, and he said to a man: Will ye give to an humble servant of God something to eat?

20 And the man said unto him: I am a Nephite, and I know that thou art a holy prophet of God, for thou art the man whom an angel said in a vision: Thou shalt receive. Therefore, go with me into my house and I will impart unto thee of my food; and I know that thou wilt be a blessing unto me and my house.

21 And it came to pass that the man received him into his house; and the man was called Amulek; and he brought forth bread and meat and set before Alma.

22 And it came to pass that Alma ate bread and was filled; and he blessed Amulek and his house, and he gave thanks unto God.

23 And after he had eaten and was filled he said unto Amulek: I am Alma, and am the high priest over the church of God throughout the land.

24 And behold, I have been called to preach the word of God among all this people, according to the spirit of revelation and prophecy; and I was in this land and they would not receive me, but they cast me out and I was about to set my back towards this land forever.

25 But behold, I have been commanded that I should turn again and prophesy unto this people, yea, and to testify against them concerning their iniquities.

26 And now, Amulek, because thou hast fed me and taken me in, thou art blessed; for I was an hungered, for I had fasted many days.

27 And Alma tarried many days with Amulek before he began to preach unto the people.

28 And it came to pass that the people did wax more gross in their iniquities.

Amulek called to preach

29 And the word came to Alma, saying: Go; and also say unto my servant Amulek, go forth and prophesy unto this people, saying—Repent ye, for thus saith the Lord, except ye repent I will visit this people in mine anger; yea, and I will not turn my fierce anger away.

The mission of Alma and Amulek

30 And Alma went forth, and also Amulek, among the people, to declare the words of God unto them; and they were filled with the Holy Ghost.

31 And they had power given unto them, insomuch that they could not be confined in dungeons; neither was it possible that any man could slay them; nevertheless they did not exercise their power until they were bound in bands and cast into prison. Now, this was done that the Lord might show forth his power in them.

32 And it came to pass that they went forth and began to preach and to prophesy unto the people, according to the spirit and power which the Lord had given them.

Amulek's testimony
Alma 10

7 As I was journeying to see a very near kindred, behold an angel of the Lord appeared unto me and said: Amulek, return to thine own house, for thou shalt feed a prophet of the Lord; yea, a holy man, who is a chosen man of God; for he has fasted many days because of the sins of this people, and he is an hungered, and thou shalt receive him into thy house and feed him, and he shall bless thee and thy house; and the blessing of the Lord shall rest upon thee and thy house.

8 And it came to pass that I obeyed the voice of the angel, and returned towards my house. And as I was going thither I found the man whom the angel said unto me: Thou shalt receive into thy house—and behold it was this same man who has been speaking unto you concerning the things of God.

9 And the angel said unto me he is a holy man; wherefore I know he is a holy man because it was said by an angel of God.

10 And again, I know that the things whereof he hath testified are true; for behold I say unto you, that as the Lord liveth, even so has he sent his angel to make these things manifest unto me; and this he has done while this Alma hath dwelt at my house.

11 For behold, he hath blessed mine house, he hath blessed me, and my women, and my children, and my father and my kinsfolk; yea, even all my kindred hath he blessed, and the blessing of the Lord hath rested upon us according to the words which he spake.

The people see

12 And now, when Amulek had spoken these words the people began to be astonished, seeing there was more than one witness who testified of the things whereof they were accused, and also of the things which were to come, according to the spirit of prophecy which was in them.

Amulek contends with Zeezrom
Alma 11

21 And this Zeezrom began to question Amulek, saying: Will ye answer me a few questions which I shall ask you? Now Zeezrom was a man who was expert in the devices of the devil, that he might destroy that which was good; therefore, he said unto Amulek: Will ye answer the questions which I shall put unto you?

22 And Amulek said unto him: Yea, if it be according to the Spirit of the Lord, which is in me; for I shall say nothing which is contrary to the Spirit of the Lord. And Zeezrom said unto him: Behold, here are six onties of silver, and all these will I give thee if thou wilt deny the existence of a Supreme Being.

23 Now Amulek said: O thou child of hell, why tempt ye me? Knowest thou that the righteous yieldeth to no such temptations?

24 Believest thou that there is no God? I say unto you, Nay, thou knowest that there is a God, but thou lovest that lucre more than him.

25 And now thou hast lied before God unto me. Thou saidst unto me—Behold these six onties, which are of great worth, I will give unto thee—when thou hadst it in thy heart to retain them from me; and it was only thy desire that I should deny the true and living God, that thou mightest have cause to destroy me. And now behold, for this great evil thou shalt have thy reward.

26 And Zeezrom said unto him: Thou sayest there is a true and living God?

27 And Amulek said: Yea, there is a true and living God.

28 Now Zeezrom said: Is there more than one God?

29 And he answered, No.

30 Now Zeezrom said unto him again: How knowest thou these things?

31 And he said: An angel hath made them known unto me.

32 And Zeezrom said again: Who is he that shall come? Is it the Son of God?

33 And he said unto him, Yea.

34 And Zeezrom said again: Shall he save his people in their sins? And Amulek answered and said unto him: I say unto you he shall not, for it is impossible for him to deny his word.

35 Now Zeezrom said unto the people: See that ye remember these things; for he said there is but one God; yet he saith that the Son of God shall come, but he shall not save his people—as though he had authority to command God.

36 Now Amulek saith again unto him: Behold thou hast lied, for thou sayest that I spake as though I had authority to command God because I said he shall not save his people in their sins.

37 And I say unto you again that he cannot save them in their sins; for I cannot deny his word, and he hath said that no unclean thing can inherit the kingdom of heaven; therefore, how can ye be saved, except ye inherit the kingdom of heaven? Therefore, ye cannot be saved in your sins.

38 Now Zeezrom saith again unto him: Is the Son of God the very Eternal Father?

39 And Amulek said unto him: Yea, he is the very Eternal Father of heaven and of earth, and all things which in them are; he is the beginning and the end, the first and the last;

40 And he shall come into the world to redeem his people; and he shall take upon him the transgressions of those who believe on his name; and these are they that shall have eternal life, and salvation cometh to none else.

41 Therefore the wicked remain as though there had been no redemption made, except it be the loosing of the bands of death; for behold, the day cometh that all shall rise from the dead and stand before God, and be judged according to their works.

42 Now, there is a death which is called a temporal death; and the death of Christ shall loose the bands of this temporal death, that all shall be raised from this temporal death.

43 The spirit and the body shall be reunited again in its perfect form; both limb and joint shall be restored to its proper frame, even as we now are at this time; and we shall be brought to stand before God, knowing even as we know now, and have a bright recollection of all our guilt.

44 Now, this restoration shall come to all, both old and young, both bond and free, both male and female, both the wicked and the righteous; and even there shall not so much as a hair of their heads be lost; but every thing shall be restored to its perfect frame, as it is now, or in the body, and shall be brought and be arraigned before the bar of Christ the Son, and God the Father, and the Holy Spirit, which is one Eternal God, to be judged according to their works, whether they be good or whether they be evil.

45 Now, behold, I have spoken unto you concerning the death of the mortal body, and also concerning the resurrection of the mortal body. I say unto you that this mortal body is raised to an immortal body, that is from death, even from the first death unto life, that they can die no more; their spirits uniting with their bodies, never to be divided; thus the whole becoming spiritual and immortal, that they can no more see corruption.

46 Now, when Amulek had finished these words the people began again to be astonished, and also Zeezrom began to tremble. And thus ended the words of Amulek, or this is all that I have written.

Alma contends with Zeezrom
Alma 12

1 Now Alma, seeing that the words of Amulek had silenced Zeezrom, for he beheld that Amulek had caught him in his lying and deceiving to destroy him, and seeing that he began to tremble under a consciousness of his guilt, he opened his mouth and began to speak unto him, and to establish the words of Amulek, and to explain things beyond, or to unfold the scriptures beyond that which Amulek had done.

2 Now the words that Alma spake unto Zeezrom were heard by the people round about; for the multitude was great, and he spake on this wise:

3 Now Zeezrom, seeing that thou hast been taken in thy lying and craftiness, for thou hast not lied unto men only but thou hast lied unto God; for behold, he knows all thy thoughts, and thou seest that thy thoughts are made known unto us by his Spirit;

4 And thou seest that we know that thy plan was a very subtle plan, as to the subtlety of the devil, for to lie and to deceive this people that thou mightest set them against us, to revile us and to cast us out—

5 Now this was a plan of thine adversary, and he hath exercised his power in thee. Now I would that ye should remember that what I say unto thee I say unto all.

6 And behold I say unto you all that this was a snare of the adversary, which he has laid to catch this people, that he might bring you into subjection unto him, that he might encircle you about with his chains, that he might chain you down to everlasting destruction, according to the power of his captivity.

7 Now when Alma had spoken these words, Zeezrom began to tremble more exceedingly, for he was convinced more and more of the power of God; and he was also convinced that Alma and Amulek had a knowledge of him, for he was convinced that they knew the thoughts and intents of his heart; for power was given unto them that they might know of these things according to the spirit of prophecy.

8 And Zeezrom began to inquire of them diligently, that he might know more concerning the kingdom of God...

Some believe
Alma 14

1 And it came to pass after he had made an end of speaking unto the people many of them did believe on his words, and began to repent, and to search the scriptures.

Others seek to destroy Alma and Amulek

2 But the more part of them were desirous that they might destroy Alma and Amulek; for they were angry with Alma, because of the plainness of his words unto Zeezrom; and they also said that Amulek had lied unto them, and had reviled against their law and also against their lawyers and judges.

3 And they were also angry with Alma and Amulek; and because they had testified so plainly against their wickedness, they sought to put them away privily.

4 But it came to pass that they did not; but they took them and bound them with strong cords, and took them before the chief judge of the land.

5 And the people went forth and witnessed against them—testifying that they had reviled against the law, and their lawyers and judges of the land, and also of all the people that were in the land; and also testified that there was but one God, and that he should send his Son among the people, but he should not save them; and many such things did the people testify against Alma and Amulek. Now this was done before the chief judge of the land.

Zeezrom repents

6 And it came to pass that Zeezrom was astonished at the words which had been spoken; and he also knew concerning the blindness of the minds, which he had caused among the people by his lying words; and his soul began to be harrowed up under a consciousness of his own guilt; yea, he began to be encircled about by the pains of hell.

Zeezrom testifies

7 And it came to pass that he began to cry unto the people, saying: Behold, I am guilty, and these men are spotless before God. And he began to plead for them from that time forth; but they reviled him, saying: Art thou also possessed with the devil?

The mob

And they spit upon him, and cast him out from among them, and also all those who believed in the words which had been spoken by Alma and Amulek; and they cast them out, and sent men to cast stones at them.

The fire

8 And they brought their wives and children together, and whosoever believed or had been taught to believe in the word of God they caused that they should be cast into the fire, and they also brought forth their records which contained the holy scriptures, and cast them into the fire also, that they might be burned and destroyed by fire.

9 And it came to pass that they took Alma and Amulek, and carried them forth to the place of martyrdom, that they might witness the destruction of those who were consumed by fire.

10 And when Amulek saw the pains of the women and children who were consuming in the fire, he also was pained; and he said unto Alma: How can we witness this awful scene? Therefore let us stretch forth our hands, and exercise the power of God which is in us, and save them from the flames.

11 But Alma said unto him: The Spirit constraineth me that I must not stretch forth mine hand; for behold the Lord receiveth them up unto himself, in glory; and he doth suffer that they may do this thing, or that the people may do this thing unto them, according to the hardness of their hearts, that the judgments which he shall exercise upon them in his wrath may be just; and the blood of the innocent shall stand as a witness against them, yea, and cry mightily against them at the last day.

12 Now Amulek said unto Alma: Behold, perhaps they will burn us also.

13 And Alma said: Be it according to the will of the Lord. But, behold, our work is not finished; therefore they burn us not.

The judgement and imprisonment

14 Now it came to pass that when the bodies of those who had been cast into the fire were consumed, and also the records which were cast in with them, the chief judge of the land came and stood before Alma and Amulek, as they were bound; and he smote them with his hand upon their cheeks, and said unto them: After what ye have seen, will ye preach again unto this people, that they shall be cast into a lake of fire and brimstone?

15 Behold, ye see that ye had not power to save those who had been cast into the fire; neither has God saved them because they were of thy faith. And the judge smote them again upon their cheeks, and asked: What say ye for yourselves?

16 Now this judge was after the order and faith of Nehor, who slew Gideon.

17 And it came to pass that Alma and Amulek answered him nothing; and he smote them again, and delivered them to the officers to be cast into prison.

18 And when they had been cast into prison three days, there came many lawyers, and judges, and priests, and teachers, who were of the profession of Nehor; and they came in unto the prison to see them, and they questioned them about many words; but they answered them nothing.

19 And it came to pass that the judge stood before them, and said: Why do ye not answer the words of this people? Know ye not that I have power to deliver you up unto the flames? And he commanded them to speak; but they answered nothing.

20 And it came to pass that they departed and went their ways, but came again on the morrow; and the judge also smote them again on their cheeks. And many came forth also, and smote them, saying: Will ye stand again and judge this people, and condemn our law? If ye have such great power why do ye not deliver yourselves?

21 And many such things did they say unto them, gnashing their teeth upon them, and spitting upon them, and saying: How shall we look when we are damned?

22 And many such things, yea, all manner of such things did they say unto them; and thus they did mock them for many days. And they did withhold food from them that they might hunger, and water that they might thirst; and they also did take from them their clothes that they were naked; and thus they were bound with strong cords, and confined in prison.

23 And it came to pass after they had thus suffered for many days, (and it was on the twelfth day, in the tenth month, in the tenth year of the reign of the judges over the people of Nephi) that the chief judge over the land of Ammonihah and many of their teachers and their lawyers went in unto the prison where Alma and Amulek were bound with cords.

24 And the chief judge stood before them, and smote them again, and said unto them: If ye have the power of God deliver yourselves from these bands, and then we will believe that the Lord will destroy this people according to your words.

25 And it came to pass that they all went forth and smote them, saying the same words, even until the last; and when the last had spoken unto them the power of God was upon Alma and Amulek, and they rose and stood upon their feet.

The Lord intervenes

26 And Alma cried, saying: How long shall we suffer these great afflictions, O Lord? O Lord, give us strength according to our faith which is in Christ, even unto deliverance. And they broke the cords with which they were bound;

The fear and destruction

and when the people saw this, they began to flee, for the fear of destruction had come upon them.

27 And it came to pass that so great was their fear that they fell to the earth, and did not obtain the outer door of the prison; and the earth shook mightily, and the walls of the prison were rent in twain, so that they fell to the earth; and the chief judge, and the lawyers, and priests, and teachers, who smote upon Alma and Amulek, were slain by the fall thereof.

28 And Alma and Amulek came forth out of the prison, and they were not hurt; for the Lord had granted unto them power, according to their faith which was in Christ. And they straightway came forth out of the prison; and they were loosed from their bands; and the prison had fallen to the earth, and every soul within the walls thereof, save it were Alma and Amulek, was slain; and they straightway came forth into the city.

29 Now the people having heard a great noise came running together by multitudes to know the cause of it; and when they saw Alma and Amulek coming forth out of the prison, and the walls thereof had fallen to the earth, they were struck with great fear, and fled from the presence of Alma and Amulek even as a goat fleeth with her young from two lions; and thus they did flee from the presence of Alma and Amulek.

The conversion and baptism of Zeezrom
Alma 15

1 And it came to pass that Alma and Amulek were commanded to depart out of that city; and they departed, and came out even into the land of Sidom; and behold, there they found all the people who had departed out of the land of Ammonihah, who had been cast out and stoned, because they believed in the words of Alma.

2 And they related unto them all that had happened unto their wives and children, and also concerning themselves, and of their power of deliverance.

3 And also Zeezrom lay sick at Sidom, with a burning fever, which was caused by the great tribulations of his mind on account of his wickedness, for he supposed that Alma and Amulek were no more; and he supposed that they had been slain because of his iniquity. And this great sin, and his many other sins, did harrow up his mind until it did become exceedingly sore, having no deliverance; therefore he began to be scorched with a burning heat.

4 Now, when he heard that Alma and Amulek were in the land of Sidom, his heart began to take courage; and he sent a message immediately unto them, desiring them to come unto him.

5 And it came to pass that they went immediately, obeying the message which he had sent unto them; and they went in unto the house unto Zeezrom; and they found him upon his bed, sick, being very low with a burning fever; and his mind also was exceedingly sore because of his iniquities; and when he saw them he stretched forth his hand, and besought them that they would heal him.

6 And it came to pass that Alma said unto him, taking him by the hand: Believest thou in the power of Christ unto salvation?

7 And he answered and said: Yea, I believe all the words that thou hast taught.

8 And Alma said: If thou believest in the redemption of Christ thou canst be healed.

9 And he said: Yea, I believe according to thy words.

10 And then Alma cried unto the Lord, saying: O Lord our God, have mercy on this man, and heal him according to his faith which is in Christ.

11 And when Alma had said these words, Zeezrom leaped upon his feet, and began to walk; and this was done to the great astonishment of all the people; and the knowledge of this went forth throughout all the land of Sidom.

12 And Alma baptized Zeezrom unto the Lord; and he began from that time forth to preach unto the people.

13 And Alma established a church in the land of Sidom, and consecrated priests and teachers in the land, to baptize unto the Lord whosoever were desirous to be baptized.

14 And it came to pass that they were many; for they did flock in from all the region round about Sidom, and were baptized.

The Mission of Ammon, a Son of Mosiah

Ammon taken before King Lamoni
Alma 17

19 And Ammon went to the land of Ishmael, the land being called after the sons of Ishmael, who also became Lamanites.

20 And as Ammon entered the land of Ishmael, the Lamanites took him and bound him, as was their custom to bind all the Nephites who fell into their hands, and carry them before the king; and thus it was left to the pleasure of the king to slay them, or to retain them in captivity, or to cast them into prison, or to cast them out of his land, according to his will and pleasure.

21 And thus Ammon was carried before the king who was over the land of Ishmael; and his name was Lamoni; and he was a descendant of Ishmael.

22 And the king inquired of Ammon if it were his desire to dwell in the land among the Lamanites, or among his people.

23 And Ammon said unto him: Yea, I desire to dwell among this people for a time; yea, and perhaps until the day I die.

24 And it came to pass that king Lamoni was much pleased with Ammon, and caused that his bands should be loosed; and he would that Ammon should take one of his daughters to wife.

Ammon defends the king's flocks

25 But Ammon said unto him: Nay, but I will be thy servant. Therefore Ammon became a servant to king Lamoni. And it came to pass that he was set among other servants to watch the flocks of Lamoni, according to the custom of the Lamanites.

26 And after he had been in the service of the king three days, as he was with the Lamanitish servants going forth with their flocks to the place of water, which was called the water of Sebus, and all the Lamanites drive their flocks hither, that they may have water—

27 Therefore, as Ammon and the servants of the king were driving forth their flocks to this place of water, behold, a certain number of the Lamanites, who had been with their flocks to water, stood and scattered the flocks of Ammon and the servants of the king, and they scattered them insomuch that they fled many ways.

28 Now the servants of the king began to murmur, saying: Now the king will slay us, as he has our brethren because their flocks were scattered by the wickedness of these men. And they began to weep exceedingly, saying: Behold, our flocks are scattered already.

29 Now they wept because of the fear of being slain. Now when Ammon saw this his heart was swollen within him with joy; for, said he, I will show forth my power unto these my fellow-servants, or the power which is in me, in restoring these flocks unto the king, that I may win the hearts of these my fellow-servants, that I may lead them to believe in my words.

30 And now, these were the thoughts of Ammon, when he saw the afflictions of those whom he termed to be his brethren.

31 And it came to pass that he flattered them by his words, saying: My brethren, be of good cheer and let us go in search of the flocks, and we will gather them together and bring them back unto the place of water; and thus we will preserve the flocks unto the king and he will not slay us.

32 And it came to pass that they went in search of the flocks, and they did follow Ammon, and they rushed forth with much swiftness and did head the flocks of the king, and did gather them together again to the place of water.

33 And those men again stood to scatter their flocks; but Ammon said unto his brethren: Encircle the flocks round about that they flee not; and I go and contend with these men who do scatter our flocks.

34 Therefore, they did as Ammon commanded them, and he went forth and stood to contend with those who stood by the waters of Sebus; and they were in number not a few.

35 Therefore they did not fear Ammon, for they supposed that one of their men could slay him according to their pleasure, for they knew not that the Lord had promised Mosiah that he would deliver his sons out of their hands; neither did they know anything concerning the Lord; therefore they delighted in the destruction of their brethren; and for this cause they stood to scatter the flocks of the king.

36 But Ammon stood forth and began to cast stones at them with his sling; yea, with mighty power he did sling stones amongst them; and thus he slew a certain number of them insomuch that they began to be astonished at his power; nevertheless they were angry because of the slain of their brethren, and they were determined that he should fall; therefore, seeing that they could not hit him with their stones, they came forth with clubs to slay him.

37 But behold, every man that lifted his club to smite Ammon, he smote off their arms with his sword; for he did withstand their blows by smiting their arms with the edge of his sword, insomuch that they began to be astonished, and began to flee before him; yea, and they were not few in number; and he caused them to flee by the strength of his arm.

38 Now six of them had fallen by the sling, but he slew none save it were their leader with his sword; and he smote off as many of their arms as were lifted against him, and they were not a few.

39 And when he had driven them afar off, he returned and they watered their flocks and returned them to the pasture of the king, and then went in unto the king, bearing the arms which had been smitten off by the sword of Ammon, of those who sought to slay him; and they were carried in unto the king for a testimony of the things which they had done.

The conversion of King Lamoni
Alma 18

1 And it came to pass that king Lamoni caused that his servants should stand forth and testify to all the things which they had seen concerning the matter.

2 And when they had all testified to the things which they had seen, and he had learned of the faithfulness of Ammon in preserving his flocks, and also of his great power in contending against those who sought to slay him, he was astonished exceedingly, and said: Surely, this is more than a man. Behold, is not this the Great Spirit who doth send such great punishments upon this people, because of their murders?

3 And they answered the king, and said: Whether he be the Great Spirit or a man, we know not; but this much we do know, that he cannot be slain by the enemies of the king; neither can they scatter the king's flocks when he is with us, because of his expertness and great strength; therefore, we know that he is a friend to the king. And now, O king, we do not believe that a man has such great power, for we know he cannot be slain.

4 And now, when the king heard these words, he said unto them: Now I know that it is the Great Spirit; and he has come down at this time to preserve your lives, that I might not slay you as I did your brethren. Now this is the Great Spirit of whom our fathers have spoken.

5 Now this was the tradition of Lamoni, which he had received from his father, that there was a Great Spirit. Notwithstanding they believed in a Great Spirit they supposed that whatsoever they did was right; nevertheless, Lamoni began to fear exceedingly, with fear lest he had done wrong in slaying his servants;

6 For he had slain many of them because their brethren had scattered their flocks at the place of water; and thus, because they had had their flocks scattered they were slain.

7 Now it was the practice of these Lamanites to stand by the waters of Sebus to scatter the flocks of the people, that thereby they might drive away many that were scattered unto their own land, it being a practice of plunder among them.

8 And it came to pass that king Lamoni inquired of his servants, saying: Where is this man that has such great power?

9 And they said unto him: Behold, he is feeding thy horses. Now the king had commanded his servants, previous to the time of the watering of their flocks, that they should prepare his horses and chariots, and conduct him forth to the land of Nephi; for there had been a great feast appointed at the land of Nephi, by the father of Lamoni, who was king over all the land.

10 Now when king Lamoni heard that Ammon was preparing his horses and his chariots he was more astonished, because of the faithfulness of Ammon, saying: Surely there has not been any servant among all my servants that has been so faithful as this man; for even he doth remember all my commandments to execute them.

11 Now I surely know that this is the Great Spirit, and I would desire him that he come in unto me, but I durst not.

12 And it came to pass that when Ammon had made ready the horses and the chariots for the king and his servants, he went in unto the king, and he saw that the countenance of the king was changed; therefore he was about to return out of his presence.

13 And one of the king's servants said unto him, Rabbanah, which is, being interpreted, powerful or great king, considering their kings to be powerful; and thus he said unto him: Rabbanah, the king desireth thee to stay.

14 Therefore Ammon turned himself unto the king, and said unto him: What wilt thou that I should do for thee, O king? And the king answered him not for the space of an hour, according to their time, for he knew not what he should say unto him.

15 And it came to pass that Ammon said unto him again: What desirest thou of me? But the king answered him not.

16 And it came to pass that Ammon, being filled with the Spirit of God, therefore he perceived the thoughts of the king. And he said unto him: Is it because thou hast heard that I defended thy servants and thy flocks, and slew seven of their brethren with the sling and with the sword, and smote off the arms of others, in order to defend thy flocks and thy servants; behold, is it this that causeth thy marvelings?

17 I say unto you, what is it, that thy marvelings are so great? Behold, I am a man, and am thy servant; therefore, whatsoever thou desirest which is right, that will I do.

18 Now when the king had heard these words, he marveled again, for he beheld that Ammon could discern his thoughts; but notwithstanding this, king Lamoni did open his mouth, and said unto him: Who art thou? Art thou that Great Spirit, who knows all things?

19 Ammon answered and said unto him: I am not.

20 And the king said: How knowest thou the thoughts of my heart? Thou mayest speak boldly, and tell me concerning these things; and also tell me by what power ye slew and smote off the arms of my brethren that scattered my flocks—

21 And now, if thou wilt tell me concerning these things, whatsoever thou desirest I will give unto thee; and if it were needed, I would guard thee with my armies; but I know that thou art more powerful than all they; nevertheless, whatsoever thou desirest of me I will grant it unto thee.

22 Now Ammon being wise, yet harmless, he said unto Lamoni: Wilt thou hearken unto my words, if I tell thee by what power I do these things? And this is the thing that I desire of thee.

23 And the king answered him, and said: Yea, I will believe all thy words. And thus he was caught with guile.

24 And Ammon began to speak unto him with boldness, and said unto him: Believest thou that there is a God?

25 And he answered, and said unto him: I do not know what that meaneth.

26 And then Ammon said: Believest thou that there is a Great Spirit?

27 And he said, Yea.

28 And Ammon said: This is God. And Ammon said unto him again: Believest thou that this Great Spirit, who is God, created all things which are in heaven and in the earth?

29 And he said: Yea, I believe that he created all things which are in the earth; but I do not know the heavens.

30 And Ammon said unto him: The heavens is a place where God dwells and all his holy angels.

31 And king Lamoni said: Is it above the earth?

32 And Ammon said: Yea, and he looketh down upon all the children of men; and he knows all the thoughts and intents of the heart; for by his hand were they all created from the beginning.

33 And king Lamoni said: I believe all these things which thou hast spoken. Art thou sent from God?

34 Ammon said unto him: I am a man; and man in the beginning was created after the image of God, and I am called by his Holy Spirit to teach these things unto this people, that they may be brought to a knowledge of that which is just and true;

35 And a portion of that Spirit dwelleth in me, which giveth me knowledge, and also power according to my faith and desires which are in God.

36 Now when Ammon had said these words, he began at the creation of the world, and also the creation of Adam, and told him all the things concerning the fall of man, and rehearsed and laid before him the records and the holy scriptures of the people, which had been spoken by the prophets, even down to the time that their father, Lehi, left Jerusalem.

37 And he also rehearsed unto them (for it was unto the king and to his servants) all the journeyings of their fathers in the wilderness, and all their sufferings with hunger and thirst, and their travail, and so forth.

38 And he also rehearsed unto them concerning the rebellions of Laman and Lemuel, and the sons of Ishmael, yea, all their rebellions did he relate unto them; and he expounded unto them all the records and scriptures from the time that Lehi left Jerusalem down to the present time.

39 But this is not all; for he expounded unto them the plan of redemption, which was prepared from the foundation of the world; and he also made known unto them concerning the coming of Christ, and all the works of the Lord did he make known unto them.

40 And it came to pass that after he had said all these things, and expounded them to the king, that the king believed all his words.

41 And he began to cry unto the Lord, saying: O Lord, have mercy; according to thy abundant mercy which thou hast had upon the people of Nephi, have upon me, and my people.

42 And now, when he had said this, he fell unto the earth, as if he were dead.

43 And it came to pass that his servants took him and carried him in unto his wife, and laid him upon a bed; and he lay as if he were dead for the space of two days and two nights; and his wife, and his sons, and his daughters mourned over him, after the manner of the Lamanites, greatly lamenting his loss.

The conversion of the queen and court
Alma 19

1 And it came to pass that after two days and two nights they were about to take his body and lay it in a sepulchre, which they had made for the purpose of burying their dead.

2 Now the queen having heard of the fame of Ammon, therefore she sent and desired that he should come in unto her.

3 And it came to pass that Ammon did as he was commanded, and went in unto the queen, and desired to know what she would that he should do.

4 And she said unto him: The servants of my husband have made it known unto me that thou art a prophet of a holy God, and that thou hast power to do many mighty works in his name;

5 Therefore, if this is the case, I would that ye should go in and see my husband, for he has been laid upon his bed for the space of two days and two nights; and some say that he is not dead, but others say that he is dead and that he stinketh, and that he ought to be placed in the sepulchre; but as for myself, to me he doth not stink.

6 Now, this was what Ammon desired, for he knew that king Lamoni was under the power of God; he knew that the dark veil of unbelief was being cast away from his mind, and the light which did light up his mind, which was the light of the glory of God, which was a marvelous light of his goodness—yea, this light had infused such joy into his soul, the cloud of darkness having been dispelled, and that the light of everlasting life was lit up in his soul, yea, he knew that this had overcome his natural frame, and he was carried away in God—

7 Therefore, what the queen desired of him was his only desire. Therefore, he went in to see the king according as the queen had desired him; and he saw the king, and he knew that he was not dead.

8 And he said unto the queen: He is not dead, but he sleepeth in God, and on the morrow he shall rise again; therefore bury him not.

9 And Ammon said unto her: Believest thou this? And she said unto him: I have had no witness save thy word, and the word of our servants; nevertheless I believe that it shall be according as thou hast said.

10 And Ammon said unto her: Blessed art thou because of thy exceeding faith; I say unto thee, woman, there has not been such great faith among all the people of the Nephites.

11 And it came to pass that she watched over the bed of her husband, from that time even until that time on the morrow which Ammon had appointed that he should rise.

12 And it came to pass that he arose, according to the words of Ammon; and as he arose, he stretched forth his hand unto the woman, and said: Blessed be the name of God, and blessed art thou.

13 For as sure as thou livest, behold, I have seen my Redeemer; and he shall come forth, and be born of a woman, and he shall redeem all mankind who believe on his name. Now, when he had said these words, his heart was swollen within him, and he sunk again with joy; and the queen also sunk down, being overpowered by the Spirit.

14 Now Ammon seeing the Spirit of the Lord poured out according to his prayers upon the Lamanites, his brethren, who had been the cause of so much mourning among the Nephites, or among all the people of God because of their iniquities and their traditions, he fell upon his knees, and began to pour out his soul in prayer and thanksgiving to God for what he had done for his brethren; and he was also overpowered with joy; and thus they all three had sunk to the earth.

15 Now, when the servants of the king had seen that they had fallen, they also began to cry unto God, for the fear of the Lord had come upon them also, for it was they who had stood before the king and testified unto him concerning the great power of Ammon.

Abish, the convert

16 And it came to pass that they did call on the name of the Lord, in their might, even until they had all fallen to the earth, save it were one of the Lamanitish women, whose name was Abish, she having been converted unto the Lord for many years, on account of a remarkable vision of her father—

17 Thus, having been converted to the Lord, and never having made it known, therefore, when she saw that all the servants of Lamoni had fallen to the earth, and also her mistress, the queen, and the king, and Ammon lay prostrate upon the earth, she knew that it was the power of God; and supposing that this opportunity, by making known unto the people what had happened among them, that by beholding this scene it would cause them to believe in the power of God, therefore she ran forth from house to house, making it known unto the people.

18 And they began to assemble themselves together unto the house of the king. And there came a multitude, and to their astonishment, they beheld the king, and the queen, and their servants prostrate upon the earth, and they all lay there as though they were dead; and they also saw Ammon, and behold, he was a Nephite.

19 And now the people began to murmur among themselves; some saying that it was a great evil that had come upon them, or upon the king and his house, because he had suffered that the Nephite should remain in the land.

20 But others rebuked them, saying: The king hath brought this evil upon his house, because he slew his servants who had had their flocks scattered at the waters of Sebus.

21 And they were also rebuked by those men who had stood at the waters of Sebus and scattered the flocks which belonged to the king, for they were angry with Ammon because of the number which he had slain of their brethren at the waters of Sebus, while defending the flocks of the king.

22 Now, one of them, whose brother had been slain with the sword of Ammon, being exceedingly angry with Ammon, drew his sword and went forth that he might let it fall upon Ammon, to slay him; and as he lifted the sword to smite him, behold, he fell dead.

23 Now we see that Ammon could not be slain, for the Lord had said unto Mosiah, his father: I will spare him, and it shall be unto him according to thy faith—therefore, Mosiah trusted him unto the Lord.

24 And it came to pass that when the multitude beheld that the man had fallen dead, who lifted the sword to slay Ammon, fear came upon them all, and they durst not put forth their hands to touch him or any of those who had fallen; and they began to marvel again among themselves what could be the cause of this great power, or what all these things could mean.

25 And it came to pass that there were many among them who said that Ammon was the Great Spirit, and others said he was sent by the Great Spirit;

26 But others rebuked them all, saying that he was a monster, who had been sent from the Nephites to torment them.

27 And there were some who said that Ammon was sent by the Great Spirit to afflict them because of their iniquities; and that it was the Great Spirit that had always attended the Nephites, who had ever delivered them out of their hands; and they said that it was this Great Spirit who had destroyed so many of their brethren, the Lamanites.

28 And thus the contention began to be exceedingly sharp among them. And while they were thus contending, the woman servant who had caused the multitude to be gathered together came, and when she saw the contention which was among the multitude she was exceedingly sorrowful, even unto tears.

29 And it came to pass that she went and took the queen by the hand, that perhaps she might raise her from the ground; and as soon as she touched her hand she arose and stood upon her feet, and cried with a loud voice, saying: O blessed Jesus, who has saved me from an awful hell! O blessed God, have mercy on this people!

30 And when she had said this, she clasped her hands, being filled with joy, speaking many words which were not understood; and when she had done this, she took the king, Lamoni, by the hand, and behold he arose and stood upon his feet.

King Lamoni preaches

31 And he, immediately, seeing the contention among his people, went forth and began to rebuke them, and to teach them the words which he had heard from the mouth of Ammon; and as many as heard his words believed, and were converted unto the Lord.

32 But there were many among them who would not hear his words; therefore they went their way.

A day of pentecost

33 And it came to pass that when Ammon arose he also administered unto them, and also did all the servants of Lamoni; and they did all declare unto the people the selfsame thing—that their hearts had been changed; that they had no more desire to do evil.

34 And behold, many did declare unto the people that they had seen angels and had conversed with them; and thus they had told them things of God, and of his righteousness.

35 And it came to pass that there were many that did believe in their words; and as many as did believe were baptized; and they became a righteous people, and they did establish a church among them.

36 And thus the work of the Lord did commence among the Lamanites; thus the Lord did begin to pour out his Spirit upon them; and we see that his arm is extended to all people who will repent and believe on his name.

King Lamoni joins Ammon on his mission
Alma 20

1 And it came to pass that when they had established a church in that land, that king Lamoni desired that Ammon should go with him to the land of Nephi, that he might show him unto his father.

2 And the voice of the Lord came to Ammon saying: Thou shalt not go up to the land of Nephi, for behold, the king will seek thy life; but thou shalt go to the land of Middoni; for behold, thy brother Aaron, and also Muloki and Ammah are in prison.

3 Now it came to pass that when Ammon had heard this, he said unto Lamoni: Behold, my brother and brethren are in prison at Middoni, and I go that I may deliver them.

4 Now Lamoni said unto Ammon: I know, in the strength of the Lord thou canst do all things. But behold, I will go with thee to the land of Middoni; for the king of the land of Middoni, whose name is Antiomno, is a friend unto me; therefore I go to the land of Middoni, that I may flatter the king of the land, and he will cast thy brethren out of prison. Now Lamoni said unto him: Who told thee that thy brethren were in prison?

5 And Ammon said unto him: No one hath told me, save it be God; and he said unto me—Go and deliver thy brethren, for they are in prison in the land of Middoni.

6 Now when Lamoni had heard this he caused that his servants should make ready his horses and his chariots.

7 And he said unto Ammon: Come, I will go with thee down to the land of Middoni, and there I will plead with the king that he will cast thy brethren out of prison.

Meeting the father of King Lamoni

8 And it came to pass that as Ammon and Lamoni were journeying thither, they met the father of Lamoni, who was king over all the land.

9 And behold, the father of Lamoni said unto him: Why did ye not come to the feast on that great day when I made a feast unto my sons, and unto my people?

10 And he also said: Whither art thou going with this Nephite, who is one of the children of a liar?

11 And it came to pass that Lamoni rehearsed unto him whither he was going, for he feared to offend him.

12 And he also told him all the cause of his tarrying in his own kingdom, that he did not go unto his father to the feast which he had prepared.

13 And now when Lamoni had rehearsed unto him all these things, behold, to his astonishment, his father was angry with him, and said: Lamoni, thou art going to deliver these Nephites, who are sons of a liar. Behold, he robbed our fathers; and now his children are also come amongst us that they may, by their cunning and their lyings, deceive us, that they again may rob us of our property.

14 Now the father of Lamoni commanded him that he should slay Ammon with the sword. And he also commanded him that he should not go to the land of Middoni, but that he should return with him to the land of Ishmael.

15 But Lamoni said unto him: I will not slay Ammon, neither will I return to the land of Ishmael, but I go to the land of Middoni that I may release the brethren of Ammon, for I know that they are just men and holy prophets of the true God.

16 Now when his father had heard these words, he was angry with him, and he drew his sword that he might smite him to the earth.

17 But Ammon stood forth and said unto him: Behold, thou shalt not slay thy son; nevertheless, it were better that he should fall than thee, for behold, he has repented of his sins; but if thou shouldst fall at this time, in thine anger, thy soul could not be saved.

18 And again, it is expedient that thou shouldst forbear; for if thou shouldst slay thy son, he being an innocent man, his blood would cry from the ground to the Lord his God, for vengeance to come upon thee; and perhaps thou wouldst lose thy soul.

19 Now when Ammon had said these words unto him, he answered him, saying: I know that if I should slay my son, that I should shed innocent blood; for it is thou that hast sought to destroy him.

20 And he stretched forth his hand to slay Ammon. But Ammon withstood his blows, and also smote his arm that he could not use it.

21 Now when the king saw that Ammon could slay him, he began to plead with Ammon that he would spare his life.

22 But Ammon raised his sword, and said unto him: Behold, I will smite thee except thou wilt grant unto me that my brethren may be cast out of prison.

The conversion of the father of King Lamoni

23 Now the king, fearing he should lose his life, said: If thou wilt spare me I will grant unto thee whatsoever thou wilt ask, even to half of the kingdom.

24 Now when Ammon saw that he had wrought upon the old king according to his desire, he said unto him: If thou wilt grant that my brethren may be cast out of prison, and also that Lamoni may retain his kingdom, and

that ye be not displeased with him, but grant that he may do according to his own desires in whatsoever thing he thinketh, then will I spare thee; otherwise I will smite thee to the earth.

25 Now when Ammon had said these words, the king began to rejoice because of his life.

26 And when he saw that Ammon had no desire to destroy him, and when he also saw the great love he had for his son Lamoni, he was astonished exceedingly, and said: Because this is all that thou hast desired, that I would release thy brethren, and suffer that my son Lamoni should retain his kingdom, behold, I will grant unto you that my son may retain his kingdom from this time and forever; and I will govern him no more—

27 And I will also grant unto thee that thy brethren may be cast out of prison, and thou and thy brethren may come unto me, in my kingdom; for I shall greatly desire to see thee. For the king was greatly astonished at the words which he had spoken, and also at the words which had been spoken by his son Lamoni, therefore he was desirous to learn them.

Ammon's imprisoned brethren freed

28 And it came to pass that Ammon and Lamoni proceeded on their journey towards the land of Middoni. And Lamoni found favor in the eyes of the king of the land; therefore the brethren of Ammon were brought forth out of prison.

29 And when Ammon did meet them he was exceedingly sorrowful, for behold they were naked, and their skins were worn exceedingly because of being bound with strong cords. And they also had suffered hunger, thirst, and all kinds of afflictions; nevertheless they were patient in all their sufferings.

30 And, as it happened, it was their lot to have fallen into the hands of a more hardened and a more stiffnecked people; therefore they would not hearken unto their words, and they had cast them out, and had smitten them, and had driven them from house to house, and from place to place, even until they had arrived in the land of Middoni; and there they were taken and cast into prison, and bound with strong cords, and kept in prison for many days, and were delivered by Lamoni and Ammon.

The Mission of Aaron, a Son of Mosiah

Aaron preaches in Jerusalem
Alma 21

1 Now when Ammon and his brethren separated themselves in the borders of the land of the Lamanites, behold Aaron took his journey towards the land which was called by the Lamanites, Jerusalem, calling it after the land of their fathers' nativity; and it was away joining the borders of Mormon.

2 Now the Lamanites and the Amalekites and the people of Amulon had built a great city, which was called Jerusalem.

3 Now the Lamanites of themselves were sufficiently hardened, but the Amalekites and the Amulonites were still harder; therefore they did cause the Lamanites that they should harden their hearts, that they should wax strong in wickedness and their abominations.

4 And it came to pass that Aaron came to the city of Jerusalem, and first began to preach to the Amalekites. And he began to preach to them in their synagogues, for they had built synagogues after the order of the Nehors; for many of the Amalekites and the Amulonites were after the order of the Nehors.

Aaron is challenged

5 Therefore, as Aaron entered into one of their synagogues to preach unto the people, and as he was speaking unto them, behold there arose an Amalekite and began to contend with him, saying: What is that thou hast testified? Hast thou seen an angel? Why do not angels appear unto us? Behold are not this people as good as thy people?

6 Thou also sayest, except we repent we shall perish. How knowest thou the thought and intent of our hearts? How knowest thou that we have cause to repent? How knowest thou that we are not a righteous people? Behold, we have built sanctuaries, and we do assemble ourselves together to worship God. We do believe that God will save all men.

Aaron opens the scriptures

7 Now Aaron said unto him: Believest thou that the Son of God shall come to redeem mankind from their sins?

8 And the man said unto him: We do not believe that thou knowest any such thing. We do not believe in these foolish traditions. We do not believe that thou knowest of things to come, neither do we believe that thy fathers and also that our fathers did know concerning the things which they spake, of that which is to come.

9 Now Aaron began to open the scriptures unto them concerning the coming of Christ, and also concerning the resurrection of the dead, and that there could be no redemption for mankind save it were through the death and sufferings of Christ, and the atonement of his blood.

10 And it came to pass as he began to expound these things unto them they were angry with him, and began to mock him; and they would not hear the words which he spake.

Aaron goes to Middoni

11 Therefore, when he saw that they would not hear his words, he departed out of their synagogue, and came over to a village which was called Ani-Anti, and there he found Muloki preaching the word unto them; and also Ammah and his brethren. And they contended with many about the word.

12 And it came to pass that they saw that the people would harden their hearts, therefore they departed and came over into the land of Middoni. And they did preach the word unto many, and few believed on the words which they taught.

Aaron is imprisoned

13 Nevertheless, Aaron and a certain number of his brethren were taken and cast into prison, and the remainder of them fled out of the land of Middoni unto the regions round about.

Aaron is delivered by King Lamoni and Ammon

14 And those who were cast into prison suffered many things, and they were delivered by the hand of Lamoni and Ammon, and they were fed and clothed.

15 And they went forth again to declare the word, and thus they were delivered for the first time out of prison; and thus they had suffered.

16 And they went forth whithersoever they were led by the Spirit of the Lord, preaching the word of God in every synagogue of the Amalekites, or in every assembly of the Lamanites where they could be admitted.

17 And it came to pass that the Lord began to bless them, insomuch that they brought many to the knowledge of the truth; yea, they did convince many of their sins, and of the traditions of their fathers, which were not correct.

Aaron teaches the father of King Lamoni
Alma 22

1 Now, as Ammon was thus teaching the people of Lamoni continually, we will return to the account of Aaron and his brethren; for after he departed from the land of Middoni he was led by the Spirit to the land of Nephi, even to the house of the king which was over all the land save it were the land of Ishmael; and he was the father of Lamoni.

2 And it came to pass that he went in unto him into the king's palace, with his brethren, and bowed himself before the king, and said unto him: Behold, O king, we are the brethren of Ammon, whom thou hast delivered out of prison.

3 And now, O king, if thou wilt spare our lives, we will be thy servants. And the king said unto them: Arise, for I will grant unto you your lives, and I will not suffer that ye shall be my servants; but I will insist that ye shall administer unto me; for I have been somewhat troubled in mind because of the generosity and the greatness of the words of thy brother Ammon; and I desire to know the cause why he has not come up out of Middoni with thee.

4 And Aaron said unto the king: Behold, the Spirit of the Lord has called him another way; he has gone to the land of Ishmael, to teach the people of Lamoni.

5 Now the king said unto them: What is this that ye have said concerning the Spirit of the Lord? Behold, this is the thing which doth trouble me.

6 And also, what is this that Ammon said—If ye will repent ye shall be saved, and if ye will not repent, ye shall be cast off at the last day?

7 And Aaron answered him and said unto him: Believest thou that there is a God? And the king said: I know that the Amalekites say that there is a God, and I have granted unto them that they should build sanctuaries, that they may assemble themselves together to worship him. And if now thou sayest there is a God, behold I will believe.

8 And now when Aaron heard this, his heart began to rejoice, and he said: Behold, assuredly as thou livest, O king, there is a God.

9 And the king said: Is God that Great Spirit that brought our fathers out of the land of Jerusalem?

10 And Aaron said unto him: Yea, he is that Great Spirit, and he created all things both in heaven and in earth. Believest thou this?

11 And he said: Yea, I believe that the Great Spirit created all things, and I desire that ye should tell me concerning all these things, and I will believe thy words.

12 And it came to pass that when Aaron saw that the king would believe his words, he began from the creation of Adam, reading the scriptures unto the king—how God created man after his own image, and that God gave him commandments, and that because of transgression, man had fallen.

13 And Aaron did expound unto him the scriptures from the creation of Adam, laying the fall of man before him, and their carnal state and also the plan of redemption, which was prepared from the foundation of the world, through Christ, for all whosoever would believe on his name.

14 And since man had fallen he could not merit anything of himself; but the sufferings and death of Christ atone for their sins, through faith and repentance, and so forth; and that he breaketh the bands of death, that the grave shall have no victory, and that the sting of death should be swallowed up in the hopes of glory; and Aaron did expound all these things unto the king.

15 And it came to pass that after Aaron had expounded these things unto him, the king said: What shall I do that I may have this eternal life of which thou hast spoken? Yea, what shall I do that I may be born of God, having this wicked spirit rooted out of my breast, and receive his Spirit, that I may be filled with joy, that I may not be cast off at the last day? Behold, said he, I will give up all that I possess, yea, I will forsake my kingdom, that I may receive this great joy.

16 But Aaron said unto him: If thou desirest this thing, if thou wilt bow down before God, yea, if thou wilt repent of all thy sins, and will bow down before God, and call on his name in faith, believing that ye shall receive, then shalt thou receive the hope which thou desirest.

The king prays

17 And it came to pass that when Aaron had said these words, the king did bow down before the Lord, upon his knees; yea, even he did prostrate himself upon the earth, and cried mightily, saying:

18 O God, Aaron hath told me that there is a God; and if there is a God, and if thou art God, wilt thou make thyself known unto me, and I will give away all my sins to know thee, and that I may be raised from the dead, and be saved at the last day. And now when the king had said these words, he was struck as if he were dead.

The queen's anger

19 And it came to pass that his servants ran and told the queen all that had happened unto the king. And she came in unto the king; and when she saw him lay as if he were dead, and also Aaron and his brethren standing as though they had been the cause of his fall, she was angry with them, and commanded that her servants, or the servants of the king, should take them and slay them.

20 Now the servants had seen the cause of the king's fall, therefore they durst not lay their hands on Aaron and his brethren; and they pled with the queen saying: Why commandest thou that we should slay these men, when behold one of them is mightier than us all? Therefore we shall fall before them.

21 Now when the queen saw the fear of the servants she also began to fear exceedingly, lest there should some evil come upon her. And she commanded her servants that they should go and call the people, that they might slay Aaron and his brethren.

Aaron raises the king

22 Now when Aaron saw the determination of the queen, he, also knowing the hardness of the hearts of the people, feared lest that a multitude should assemble themselves together, and there should be a great contention and a disturbance among them; therefore he put forth his hand and raised the king from the earth, and said unto him: Stand. And he stood upon his feet, receiving his strength.

23 Now this was done in the presence of the queen and many of the servants. And when they saw it they greatly marveled, and began to fear. And the king stood forth, and began to minister unto them. And he did minister unto them, insomuch that his whole household were converted unto the Lord.

24 Now there was a multitude gathered together because of the commandment of the queen, and there began to be great murmurings among them because of Aaron and his brethren.

25 But the king stood forth among them and administered unto them. And they were pacified towards Aaron and those who were with him.

26 And it came to pass that when the king saw that the people were pacified, he caused that Aaron and his brethren should stand forth in the midst of the multitude, and that they should preach the word unto them.

27 And it came to pass that the king sent a proclamation throughout all the land...

The Mission of Nephi and Lehi, the Sons of Helaman

The commitment
Helaman 5

4 And it came to pass that Nephi had become weary because of their iniquity; and he yielded up the judgment-seat, and took it upon him to preach the word of God all the remainder of his days, and his brother Lehi also, all the remainder of his days;

Father Helaman's counsel

5 For they remembered the words which their father Helaman spake unto them. And these are the words which he spake:

The names of our first parents

6 Behold, my sons, I desire that ye should remember to keep the commandments of God; and I would that ye should declare unto the people these words. Behold, I have given unto you the names of our first parents who came out of the land of Jerusalem; and this I have done that when you remember your names ye may remember them; and when ye remember them ye may remember their works; and when ye remember their works ye may know how that it is said, and also written, that they were good.

7 Therefore, my sons, I would that ye should do that which is good, that it may be said of you, and also written, even as it has been said and written of them.

8 And now my sons, behold I have somewhat more to desire of you, which desire is, that ye may not do these things that ye may boast, but that ye may do these things to lay up for yourselves a treasure in heaven, yea, which is eternal, and which fadeth not away; yea, that ye may have that precious gift of eternal life, which we have reason to suppose hath been given to our fathers.

Remember King Benjamin

9 O remember, remember, my sons, the words which king Benjamin spake unto his people; yea, remember that there is no other way nor means whereby man can be saved, only through the atoning blood of Jesus Christ, who shall come, yea, remember that he cometh to redeem the world.

Remember Amulek and Zeezrom

10 And remember also the words which Amulek spake unto Zeezrom, in the city of Ammonihah; for he said unto him that the Lord surely should come to redeem his people, but that he should not come to redeem them in their sins, but to redeem them from their sins.

11 And he hath power given unto him from the Father to redeem them from their sins because of repentance; therefore he hath sent his angels to declare the tidings of the conditions of repentance, which bringeth unto the power of the Redeemer, unto the salvation of their souls.

Remember Christ

12 And now, my sons, remember, remember that it is upon the rock of our Redeemer, who is Christ, the Son of God, that ye must build your foundation; that when the devil shall send forth his mighty winds, yea, his shafts in the whirlwind, yea, when all his hail and his mighty storm shall beat upon you, it shall have no power over you to drag you down to the gulf of misery and endless wo, because of the rock upon which ye are built, which is a sure foundation, a foundation whereon if men build they cannot fall.

shall send forth his mighty winds, yea, his shafts in the whirlwind, yea, when all his hail and his mighty storm shall beat upon you, it shall have no power over you to drag you down to the gulf of misery and endless wo, because of the rock upon which ye are built, which is a sure foundation, a foundation whereon if men build they cannot fall.

13 And it came to pass that these were the words which Helaman taught to his sons; yea, he did teach them many things which are not written, and also many things which are written.

Teaching the Nephites

14 And they did remember his words; and therefore they went forth, keeping the commandments of God, to teach the word of God among all the people of Nephi, beginning at the city Bountiful;

15 And from thenceforth to the city of Gid; and from the city of Gid to the city of Mulek;

16 And even from one city to another, until they had gone forth among all the people of Nephi who were in the land southward; and from thence into the land of Zarahemla, among the Lamanites.

17 And it came to pass that they did preach with great power, insomuch that they did confound many of those dissenters who had gone over from the Nephites, insomuch that they came forth and did confess their sins and were baptized unto repentance, and immediately returned to the Nephites to endeavor to repair unto them the wrongs which they had done.

Teaching the Lamanites

18 And it came to pass that Nephi and Lehi did preach unto the Lamanites with such great power and authority, for they had power and authority, given unto them that they might speak, and they also had what they should speak given unto them—

19 Therefore they did speak unto the great astonishment of the Lamanites, to the convincing them, insomuch that there were eight thousand of the Lamanites who were in the land of Zarahemla and round about baptized unto repentance, and were convinced of the wickedness of the traditions of their fathers.

In the land of Nephi

20 And it came to pass that Nephi and Lehi did proceed from thence to go to the land of Nephi.

Imprisoned

21 And it came to pass that they were taken by an army of the Lamanites and cast into prison; yea, even in that same prison in which Ammon and his brethren were cast by the servants of Limhi.

22 And after they had been cast into prison many days without food, behold, they went forth into the prison to take them that they might slay them.

Encircled by fire

23 And it came to pass that Nephi and Lehi were encircled about as if by fire, even insomuch that they durst not lay their hands upon them for fear lest they should be burned. Nevertheless, Nephi and Lehi were not burned; and they were as standing in the midst of fire and were not burned.

24 And when they saw that they were encircled about with a pillar of fire, and that it burned them not, their hearts did take courage.

25 For they saw that the Lamanites durst not lay their hands upon them; neither durst they come near unto them, but stood as if they were struck dumb with amazement.

26 And it came to pass that Nephi and Lehi did stand forth and began to speak unto them, saying: Fear not, for behold, it is God that has shown unto you this marvelous thing, in the which is shown unto you that ye cannot lay your hands on us to slay us.

27 And behold, when they had said these words, the earth shook exceedingly, and the walls of the prison did shake as if they were about to tumble to the earth; but behold, they did not fall. And behold, they that were in

the prison were Lamanites and Nephites who were dissenters.

28 And it came to pass that they were overshadowed with a cloud of darkness, and an awful solemn fear came upon them.

The voice of the Lord

29 And it came to pass that there came a voice as if it were above the cloud of darkness, saying: Repent ye, repent ye, and seek no more to destroy my servants whom I have sent unto you to declare good tidings.

30 And it came to pass when they heard this voice, and beheld that it was not a voice of thunder, neither was it a voice of a great tumultuous noise, but behold, it was a still voice of perfect mildness, as if it had been a whisper, and it did pierce even to the very soul—

31 And notwithstanding the mildness of the voice, behold the earth shook exceedingly, and the walls of the prison trembled again, as if it were about to tumble to the earth; and behold the cloud of darkness, which had overshadowed them, did not disperse—

32 And behold the voice came again, saying: Repent ye, repent ye, for the kingdom of heaven is at hand; and seek no more to destroy my servants. And it came to pass that the earth shook again, and the walls trembled.

33 And also again the third time the voice came, and did speak unto them marvelous words which cannot be uttered by man; and the walls did tremble again, and the earth shook as if it were about to divide asunder.

34 And it came to pass that the Lamanites could not flee because of the cloud of darkness which did overshadow them; yea, and also they were immovable because of the fear which did come upon them.

Aminadab, the less active

35 Now there was one among them who was a Nephite by birth, who had once belonged to the church of God but had dissented from them.

36 And it came to pass that he turned him about, and behold, he saw through the cloud of darkness the faces of Nephi and Lehi; and behold, they did shine exceedingly, even as the faces of angels. And he beheld that they did lift their eyes to heaven; and they were in the attitude as if talking or lifting their voices to some being whom they beheld.

37 And it came to pass that this man did cry unto the multitude, that they might turn and look. And behold, there was power given unto them that they did turn and look; and they did behold the faces of Nephi and Lehi.

38 And they said unto the man: Behold, what do all these things mean, and who is it with whom these men do converse?

39 Now the man's name was Aminadab. And Aminadab said unto them: They do converse with the angels of God.

40 And it came to pass that the Lamanites said unto him: What shall we do, that this cloud of darkness may be removed from overshadowing us?

41 And Aminadab said unto them: You must repent, and cry unto the voice, even until ye shall have faith in Christ, who was taught unto you by Alma, and Amulek, and Zeezrom; and when ye shall do this, the cloud of darkness shall be removed from overshadowing you.

The Lamanites repent

42 And it came to pass that they all did begin to cry unto the voice of him who had shaken the earth; yea, they did cry even until the cloud of darkness was dispersed.

43 And it came to pass that when they cast their eyes about, and saw that the cloud of darkness was dispersed from overshadowing them, behold, they saw that they were encircled about, yea every soul, by a pillar of fire.

44 And Nephi and Lehi were in the midst of them; yea, they were encircled about; yea, they were as if in the midst of a flaming fire, yet it did harm them not, neither did it take hold upon the walls of the prison; and they were filled with that joy which is unspeakable and full of glory.

The Holy Spirit of God

45 And behold, the Holy Spirit of God did come down from heaven, and did enter into their hearts, and they were filled as if with fire, and they could speak forth marvelous words.

A voice

46 And it came to pass that there came a voice unto them, yea, a pleasant voice, as if it were a whisper, saying:

47 Peace, peace be unto you, because of your faith in my Well Beloved, who was from the foundation of the world.

Angels

48 And now, when they heard this they cast up their eyes as if to behold from whence the voice came; and behold, they saw the heavens open; and angels came down out of heaven and ministered unto them.

49 And there were about three hundred souls who saw and heard these things; and they were bidden to go forth and marvel not, neither should they doubt.

The Lamanites are converted

50 And it came to pass that they did go forth, and did minister unto the people, declaring throughout all the regions round about all the things which they had heard and seen, insomuch that the more part of the Lamanites were convinced of them, because of the greatness of the evidences which they had received.

51 And as many as were convinced did lay down their weapons of war, and also their hatred and the tradition of their fathers.

52 And it came to pass that they did yield up unto the Nephites the lands of their possession.

The Mission of Samuel the Lamanite

Nephites wicked, Lamanites righteous
Helaman 13

1 And now it came to pass in the eighty and sixth year, the Nephites did still remain in wickedness, yea, in great wickedness, while the Lamanites did observe strictly to keep the commandments of God, according to the law of Moses.

Samuel the Lamanite preaches to the Nephites

2 And it came to pass that in this year there was one Samuel, a Lamanite, came into the land of Zarahemla, and began to preach unto the people. And it came to pass that he did preach, many days, repentance unto the people, and they did cast him out, and he was about to return to his own land.

The Lord speaks to Samuel

3 But behold, the voice of the Lord came unto him, that he should return again, and prophesy unto the people whatsoever things should come into his heart.

On the wall

4 And it came to pass that they would not suffer that he should enter into the city; therefore he went and got upon the wall thereof, and stretched forth his hand and cried with a loud voice, and prophesied unto the people whatsoever things the Lord put into his heart.

5 And he said unto them: Behold, I, Samuel, a Lamanite, do speak the words of the Lord which he doth put into my heart; and behold he hath put it into my heart to say unto this people that the sword of justice hangeth over this people; and four hundred years pass not away save the sword of justice falleth upon this people.

6 Yea, heavy destruction awaiteth this people, and it surely cometh unto this people, and nothing can save this people save it be repentance and faith on the Lord Jesus Christ, who surely shall come into the world, and shall suffer many things and shall be slain for his people.

7 And behold, an angel of the Lord hath declared it unto me, and he did bring glad tidings to my soul. And behold, I was sent unto you to declare it unto you also, that ye might have glad tidings; but behold ye would not receive me.

8 Therefore, thus saith the Lord: Because of the hardness of the hearts of the people of the Nephites, except they repent I will take away my word from them, and I will withdraw my Spirit from them, and I will suffer them no longer, and I will turn the hearts of their brethren against them.

400 years

9 And four hundred years shall not pass away before I will cause that they shall be smitten; yea, I will visit them with the sword and with famine and with pestilence.

10 Yea, I will visit them in my fierce anger, and there shall be those of the fourth generation who shall live, of your enemies, to behold your utter destruction; and this shall surely come except ye repent, saith the Lord; and those of the fourth generation shall visit your destruction.

11 But if ye will repent and return unto the Lord your God I will turn away mine anger, saith the Lord; yea, thus saith the Lord, blessed are they who will repent and turn unto me, but wo unto him that repenteth not.

Wo unto Zarahemla

12 Yea, wo unto this great city of Zarahemla; for behold, it is because of those who are righteous that it is saved; yea, wo unto this great city, for I perceive, saith the Lord, that there are many, yea, even the more part of this great city, that will harden their hearts against me, saith the Lord.

13 But blessed are they who will repent, for them will I spare. But behold, if it were not for the righteous who are in this great city, behold, I would cause that fire should come down out of heaven and destroy it.

14 But behold, it is for the righteous' sake that it is spared. But behold, the time cometh, saith the Lord, that when ye shall cast out the righteous from among you, then shall ye be ripe for destruction; yea, wo be unto this great city, because of the wickedness and abominations which are in her.

Wo unto Gideon

15 Yea, and wo be unto the city of Gideon, for the wickedness and abominations which are in her.

16 Yea, and wo be unto all the cities which are in the land round about, which are possessed by the Nephites, because of the wickedness and abominations which are in them.

17 And behold, a curse shall come upon the land, saith the Lord of Hosts, because of the people's sake who are upon the land, yea, because of their wickedness and their abominations.

Hiding up treasures

18 And it shall come to pass, saith the Lord of Hosts, yea, our great and true God, that whoso shall hide up treasures in the earth shall find them again no more, because of the great curse of the land, save he be a righteous man and shall hide it up unto the Lord.

19 For I will, saith the Lord, that they shall hide up their treasures unto me; and cursed be they who hide not up their treasures unto me; for none hideth up their treasures unto me save it be the righteous; and he that hideth not up his treasures unto me, cursed is he, and also the treasure, and none shall redeem it because of the curse of the land.

20 And the day shall come that they shall hide up their treasures, because they have set their hearts upon riches; and because they have set their hearts upon their riches, and will hide up their treasures when they shall flee before their enemies; because they will not hide them up unto me, cursed be they and also their treasures; and in that day shall they be smitten, saith the Lord.

Cursed because of riches

21 Behold ye, the people of this great city, and hearken unto my words; yea, hearken unto the words which the Lord saith; for behold, he saith that ye are cursed because of your riches, and also are your riches cursed because ye have set your hearts upon them, and have not hearkened unto the words of him who gave them unto you.

22 Ye do not remember the Lord your God in the things with which he hath blessed you, but ye do always remember your riches, not to thank the Lord your God for them; yea, your hearts are not drawn out unto the Lord, but they do swell with great pride, unto boasting, and unto great swelling, envyings, strifes, malice, persecutions and murders, and all manner of iniquities.

23 For this cause hath the Lord God caused that a curse should come upon the land, and also upon your riches, and this because of your iniquities.

Cast out the prophets

24 Yea, wo unto this people, because of this time which has arrived, that ye do cast out the prophets, and do mock them, and cast stones at them, and do slay them, and do all manner of iniquity unto them, even as they did of old time.

25 And now when ye talk, ye say: If our days had been in the days of our fathers of old, we would not have slain the prophets; we would not have stoned them, and cast them out.

26 Behold ye are worse than they; for as the Lord liveth, if a prophet come among you and declareth unto you the word of the Lord, which testifieth of your sins and iniquities, ye are angry with him, and cast him out and seek all manner of ways to destroy him; yea, you will say that he is a false prophet, and that he is a sinner, and of the devil, because he testifieth that your deeds are evil.

27 But behold, if a man shall come among you and shall say: Do this, and there is no iniquity; do that and ye shall not suffer; yea, he will say: Walk after the pride of your own hearts; yea, walk after the pride of your eyes, and do whatsoever your heart desireth—and if a man shall come among you and say this, ye will receive him, and say that he is a prophet.

28 Yea, ye will lift him up, and ye will give unto him of your substance; ye will give unto him of your gold, and of your silver, and ye will clothe him with costly apparel; and because he speaketh flattering words unto you, and he saith that all is well, then ye will not find fault with him.

Wicked and perverse generation

29 O ye wicked and ye perverse generation; ye hardened and ye stiffnecked people, how long will ye suppose that the Lord will suffer you? Yea, how long will ye suffer yourselves to be led by foolish and blind guides? Yea, how long will ye choose darkness rather than light?

Destruction made sure

30 Yea, behold, the anger of the Lord is already kindled against you; behold, he hath cursed the land because of your iniquity.

31 And behold, the time cometh that he curseth your riches, that they become slippery, that ye cannot hold them; and in the days of your poverty ye cannot retain them.

32 And in the days of your poverty ye shall cry unto the Lord; and in vain shall ye cry, for your desolation is already come upon you, and your destruction is made sure; and then shall ye weep and howl in that day, saith the Lord of Hosts. And then shall ye lament, and say:

O that I had repented

33 O that I had repented, and had not killed the prophets, and stoned them, and cast them out. Yea, in that day ye shall say: O that we had remembered the Lord our God in the day that he gave us our riches, and then they would not have become slippery that we should lose them; for behold, our riches are gone from us.

34 Behold, we lay a tool here and on the morrow it is gone; and behold, our swords are taken from us in the day we have sought them for battle.

35 Yea, we have hid up our treasures and they have slipped away from us, because of the curse of the land.

36 O that we had repented in the day that the word of the Lord came unto us; for behold the land is cursed, and all things are become slippery, and we cannot hold them.

37 Behold, we are surrounded by demons, yea, we are encircled about by the angels of him who hath sought to destroy our souls. Behold, our iniquities are great. O Lord, canst thou not turn away thine anger from us? And this shall be your language in those days.

Procrastinated until everlastingly too late

38 But behold, your days of probation are past; ye have procrastinated the day of your salvation until it is everlastingly too late, and your destruction is made sure; yea, for ye have sought all the days of your lives for that which ye could not obtain; and ye have sought for happiness in doing iniquity, which thing is contrary to the nature of that righteousness which is in our great and Eternal Head.

39 O ye people of the land, that ye would hear my words! And I pray that the anger of the Lord be turned away from you, and that ye would repent and be saved.

Helaman 14

1 And now it came to pass that Samuel, the Lamanite, did prophesy a great many more things which cannot be written.

A sign of his coming

2 And behold, he said unto them: Behold, I give unto you a sign; for five years more cometh, and behold, then cometh the Son of God to redeem all those who shall believe on his name.

3 And behold, this will I give unto you for a sign at the time of his coming; for behold, there shall be great lights in heaven, insomuch that in the night before he cometh there shall be no darkness, insomuch that it shall appear unto man as if it was day.

4 Therefore, there shall be one day and a night and a day, as if it were one day and there were no night; and this shall be unto you for a sign; for ye shall know of the rising of the sun and also of its setting; therefore they shall know of a surety that there shall be two days and a night; nevertheless the night shall not be darkened; and it shall be the night before he is born.

5 And behold, there shall a new star arise, such an one as ye never have beheld; and this also shall be a sign unto you.

6 And behold this is not all, there shall be many signs and wonders in heaven.

7 And it shall come to pass that ye shall all be amazed, and wonder, insomuch that ye shall fall to the earth.

8 And it shall come to pass that whosoever shall believe on the Son of God, the same shall have everlasting life.

9 And behold, thus hath the Lord commanded me, by his angel, that I should come and tell this thing unto you; yea, he hath commanded that I should prophesy these things unto you; yea, he hath said unto me: Cry unto this people, repent and prepare the way of the Lord.

Because I am a Lamanite

10 And now, because I am a Lamanite, and have spoken unto you the words which the Lord hath commanded me, and because it was hard against you, ye are angry with me and do seek to destroy me, and have cast me out from among you.

11 And ye shall hear my words, for, for this intent have I come up upon the walls of this city, that ye might hear and know of the judgments of God which do await you because of your iniquities, and also that ye might know the conditions of repentance;

Might know and believe

12 And also that ye might know of the coming of Jesus Christ, the Son of God, the Father of heaven and of earth, the Creator of all things from the beginning; and that ye might know of the signs of his coming, to the intent that ye might believe on his name.

13 And if ye believe on his name ye will repent of all your sins, that thereby ye may have a remission of them through his merits.

Salvation and resurrection

14 And behold, again, another sign I give unto you, yea, a sign of his death.

15 For behold, he surely must die that salvation may come; yea, it behooveth him and becometh expedient that he dieth, to bring to pass the resurrection of the dead, that thereby men may be brought into the presence of the Lord.

16 Yea, behold, this death bringeth to pass the resurrection, and redeemeth all mankind from the first death—that spiritual death; for all mankind, by the fall of Adam being cut off from the presence of the Lord, are considered as dead, both as to things temporal and to things spiritual.

17 But behold, the resurrection of Christ redeemeth mankind, yea, even all mankind, and bringeth them back into the presence of the Lord.

18 Yea, and it bringeth to pass the condition of repentance, that whosoever repenteth the same is not hewn down and cast into the fire; but whosoever repenteth not is hewn down and cast into the fire; and there cometh upon them again a spiritual death, yea, a second death, for they are cut off again as to things pertaining to righteousness.

19 Therefore repent ye, repent ye, lest by knowing these things and not doing them ye shall suffer yourselves to come under condemnation, and ye are brought down unto this second death.

A sign of his death

20 But behold, as I said unto you concerning another sign, a sign of his death, behold, in that day that he shall suffer death the sun shall be darkened and refuse to give his light unto you; and also the moon and the stars; and there shall be no light upon the face of this land, even from the time that he shall suffer death, for the space of three days, to the time that he shall rise again from the dead.

21 Yea, at the time that he shall yield up the ghost there shall be thunderings and lightnings for the space of many hours, and the earth shall shake and tremble; and the rocks which are upon the face of this earth, which are both above the earth and beneath, which ye know at this time are solid, or the more part of it is one solid mass, shall be broken up;

22 Yea, they shall be rent in twain, and shall ever after be found in seams and in cracks, and in broken fragments upon the face of the whole earth, yea, both above the earth and beneath.

23 And behold, there shall be great tempests, and there shall be many mountains laid low, like unto a valley, and there shall be many places which are now called valleys which shall become mountains, whose height is great.

24 And many highways shall be broken up, and many cities shall become desolate.

25 And many graves shall be opened, and shall yield up many of their dead; and many saints shall appear unto many.

26 And behold, thus hath the angel spoken unto me; for he said unto me that there should be thunderings and lightnings for the space of many hours.

27 And he said unto me that while the thunder and the lightning lasted, and the tempest, that these things should be, and that darkness should cover the face of the whole earth for the space of three days.

28 And the angel said unto me that many shall see greater things than these, to the intent that they might believe that these signs and these wonders should come to pass upon all the face of this land, to the intent that there should be no cause for unbelief among the children of men—

Believe or perish

29 And this to the intent that whosoever will believe might be saved, and that whosoever will not believe, a righteous judgment might come upon them; and also if they are condemned they bring upon themselves their own condemnation.

30 And now remember, remember, my brethren, that whosoever perisheth, perisheth unto himself; and whosoever doeth iniquity, doeth it unto himself; for behold, ye are free; ye are permitted to act for yourselves; for behold, God hath given unto you a knowledge and he hath made you free.

31 He hath given unto you that ye might know good from evil, and he hath given unto you that ye might choose life or death; and ye can do good and be restored unto that which is good, or have that which is good restored unto you; or ye can do evil, and have that which is evil restored unto you.

Houses and women
Helaman 15

1 And now, my beloved brethren, behold, I declare unto you that except ye shall repent your houses shall be left unto you desolate.

2 Yea, except ye repent, your women shall have great cause to mourn in the day that they shall give suck; for ye shall attempt to flee and there shall be no place for refuge; yea, and wo unto them which are with child, for they shall be heavy and cannot flee; therefore, they shall be trodden down and shall be left to perish.

The Nephites he hath loved

3 Yea, wo unto this people who are called the people of Nephi except they shall repent, when they shall see all these signs and wonders which shall be showed unto them; for behold, they have been a chosen people of the Lord; yea, the people of Nephi hath he loved, and also hath he chastened them; yea, in the days of their iniquities hath he chastened them because he loveth them.

Salvation of the Lamanites

4 But behold my brethren, the Lamanites hath he hated because their deeds have been evil continually, and this because of the iniquity of the tradition of their fathers. But behold, salvation hath come unto them through the preaching of the Nephites; and for this intent hath the Lord prolonged their days.

5 And I would that ye should behold that the more part of them are in the path of their duty, and they do walk circumspectly before God, and they do observe to keep his commandments and his statutes and his judgments according to the law of Moses.

6 Yea, I say unto you, that the more part of them are doing this, and they are striving with unwearied diligence that they may bring the remainder of their brethren to the knowledge of the truth; therefore there are many who do add to their numbers daily.

7 And behold, ye do know of yourselves, for ye have witnessed it, that as many of them as are brought to the knowledge of the truth, and to know of the wicked and abominable traditions of their fathers, and are led to believe the holy scriptures, yea, the prophecies of the holy prophets, which are written, which leadeth them to faith on the Lord, and unto repentance, which faith and repentance bringeth a change of heart unto them—

8 Therefore, as many as have come to this, ye know of yourselves are firm and steadfast in the faith, and in the thing wherewith they have been made free.

9 And ye know also that they have buried their weapons of war, and they fear to take them up lest by any means they should sin; yea, ye can see that they fear to sin—for behold they will suffer themselves that they be trodden down and slain by their enemies, and will not lift their swords against them, and this because of their faith in Christ.

10 And now, because of their steadfastness when they do believe in that thing which they do believe, for because of their firmness when they are once enlightened, behold, the Lord shall bless them and prolong their days, notwithstanding their iniquity—

11 Yea, even if they should dwindle in unbelief the Lord shall prolong their days, until the time shall come which hath been spoken of by our fathers, and also by the prophet Zenos, and many other prophets, concerning the restoration of our brethren, the Lamanites, again to the knowledge of the truth—

12 Yea, I say unto you, that in the latter times the promises of the Lord have been extended to our brethren, the Lamanites; and notwithstanding the many afflictions which they shall have, and notwithstanding they shall be driven to and fro upon the face of the earth, and be hunted, and shall be smitten and scattered abroad, having no place for refuge, the Lord shall be merciful unto them.

13 And this is according to the prophecy, that they shall again be brought to the true knowledge, which is the knowledge of their Redeemer, and their great and true shepherd, and be numbered among his sheep.

Better for them than you

14 Therefore I say unto you, it shall be better for them than for you except ye repent.

15 For behold, had the mighty works been shown unto them which have been shown unto you, yea, unto them who have dwindled in unbelief because of the traditions of their fathers, ye can see of yourselves that they never would again have dwindled in unbelief.

16 Therefore, saith the Lord: I will not utterly destroy them, but I will cause that in the day of my wisdom they shall return again unto me, saith the Lord.

17 And now behold, saith the Lord, concerning the people of the Nephites: If they will not repent, and observe to do my will, I will utterly destroy them, saith the Lord, because of their unbelief notwithstanding the many mighty works which I have done among them; and as surely as the Lord liveth shall these things be, saith the Lord.

Many believed
Helaman 16

1 And now, it came to pass that there were many who heard the words of Samuel, the Lamanite, which he spake upon the walls of the city. And as many as believed on his word went forth and sought for Nephi; and when they had come forth and found him they confessed unto him their sins and denied not, desiring that they might be baptized unto the Lord.

Many did not

2 But as many as there were who did not believe in the words of Samuel were angry with him; and they cast stones at him upon the wall, and also many shot arrows at him as he stood upon the wall; but the Spirit of the Lord was with him, insomuch that they could not hit him with their stones neither with their arrows.

3 Now when they saw that they could not hit him, there were many more who did believe on his words, insomuch that they went away unto Nephi to be baptized.

Nephi baptizing

4 For behold, Nephi was baptizing, and prophesying, and preaching, crying repentance unto the people, showing signs and wonders, working miracles among the people, that they might know that the Christ must shortly come—

5 Telling them of things which must shortly come, that they might know and remember at the time of their coming that they had been made known unto them beforehand, to the intent that they might believe; therefore as many as believed on the words of Samuel went forth unto him to be baptized, for they came repenting and confessing their sins.

We cannot hit him

6 But the more part of them did not believe in the words of Samuel; therefore when they saw that they could not hit him with their stones and their arrows, they cried unto their captains, saying: Take this fellow and bind him, for behold he hath a devil; and because of the power of the devil which is in him we cannot hit him with our stones and our arrows; therefore take him and bind him, and away with him.

7 And as they went forth to lay their hands on him, behold, he did cast himself down from the wall, and did flee out of their lands, yea, even unto his own country, and began to preach and to prophesy among his own people.

8 And behold, he was never heard of more among the Nephites; and thus were the affairs of the people.

Stories

A Golden Referral

One day in the autumn of 1966, I participated in an exchange of companions with my district leader. From my area in Jamestown, New York, I went with Elder Brown to his area in Meadville, Pennsylvania.

It was late afternoon as we drove along visiting and laughing about past missionary companions and experiences.

Midway through our trip, I saw a road sign indicating that we were approaching Corry, Pennsylvania. I remembered receiving a referral to a family there by the name of Testi, but we hadn't made contact because we had expended our limited miles. I asked Elder Brown if he minded stopping while I rummaged through my briefcase for the information.

In those days, there wasn't much in Corry. We stopped at a rural gas station with a small farm and home next door to ask directions. As luck (or the Lord) would have it, Mr. Testi owned the gas station. He invited us to stay for a visit and then he went off to gather his family.

Expecting the man and his family to return at any moment, we waited and waited and waited. Finally, the entire Testi family appeared, freshly scrubbed and in their Sunday best, to meet the Mormon missionaries. Mr. Testi closed the gas station so we could talk without interruption.

As missionaries, we always hope the Spirit attends us. The Testis came to us already possessing the Spirit.

While visiting, we were surprised to learn that the Testis had vacationed in Utah earlier that summer. Somewhere near Provo-Orem, one of their suitcases had blown off the top of their car—which they had not realize until they had reached Salt Lake.

The Testis called the police, only to learn that a family in Orem had found the suitcase and had notified the police in case anyone contacted the police looking for it.

The Testis drove to Orem to retrieve their suitcase from the first LDS family they had ever met. They stayed for dinner and were invited by the family to visit Temple Square—where they filled out a card inviting the missionaries to call on them at their home in Pennsylvania.

While we were presenting the first discussion, we learned that the family had already purchased a Book of Mormon and that Mr. Testi had already read it.

Our first discussion was wonderful. We concluded with prayer and invited the Testis to attend church with us the following Sunday.

It was quite a distance for them to drive to Jamestown to attend Sunday School—which, in those days, was held in the morning. Much to our embarrassment, the Gospel Essentials teacher—the class to where we normally took our investigators—didn't show up.

Surprisingly, Mr. Testi had read something about the lesson subject matter in the Book of Mormon and proceeded to lead a group discussion—that also allowed him to ask questions about the church and gospel. A lively time was had by all!

In those days, sacrament meeting was held in the evening. We did not expect the Testis to make the long drive again—but they did!

Several miracles happened while we were teaching this wonderful family, but they were all baptized, on time, and with many members attending the baptismal service.

Since then, Bro. Testi has served in the branch and district presidencies; Sis. Testi has served in almost all the auxiliaries; a young son has served a mission; all the children have been married in the temple; and, after retiring, Bro. and Sis. Testi served a mission together.

—*Stan Miller*

From 20 People to 2 Stakes

In 1970, I spent the last two months of my mission in Huehuetenango (pronounced: way-way-ta-non-go), Guatemala, with Elder Evans, with whom I had entered the mission field almost two years earlier.

Huehuetenango was a beautiful small town way up in the mountains near the Mexican border. There were approximately 500 church members in the area, but only about 20 of them were active.

Elder Evans and I both worked hard and had a lot of fun in Huehuetenango. We loved the sweet, humble people, who we knew to be the descendants of Lehi.

While there, Elder Evans and I were blessed to baptize and confirm 10 new church members in the area. Naturally, we hoped all would stay active. Realistically, we knew as few as 1 or 2 would. I never did learn how many of our converts remained active.

My mission ended, I toured the Book of Mormon ruins in Mexico, returned home, and got on with my life.

Twenty-six years later, I was reading the *New Stakes Created* section of the *LDS Church News* when I noticed that a second stake had been created in Huehuetenango. I read the news again and again. I could not believe it. Tears came to my eyes.

A stake typically includes 2,500 people. Twenty-six years ago, Huehuetenango had only 20 active members. Now, there were two stakes with more than 5,000 people. I would never have believed that could happen in that small mountain town.

I keep the clipping of that news story in my scriptures to remind me of how fast the church can grow in an area once it gets a foot-hold. I am reminded of the scripture in Doctrine and Covenants 65:2:

> *The keys of the kingdom of God are committed unto man on the earth, and from thence shall the gospel roll forth unto the ends of the earth, as the stone which is cut out of the mountain without hands shall roll forth, until it has filled the whole earth.*

Not only have I witnessed a partial fulfillment of that prophecy in my lifetime, but I saw it with my own eyes, and helped with my own hands. It humbles me still.

—*Sherm Fugal*

❧

The Miraculous Mission of Elder David W. Taylor

Some 30 years ago, Elder David W. Taylor, of Mesa, Arizona, served a mission in the New York Cumorah Mission (now New York Rochester Mission) of the Church of Jesus Christ of Latter-day Saints, where the church was originally restored and organized.

Though it sounds like a romantic, if not easy, mission, it is not. The church struggled in western New York in its early days and continues to struggle today with few baptisms, and more branches than wards.

Recently, the former Elder Taylor logged on to the Cumorah Mission website and noted a family name—Ball—that he remembered from his missionary experience. He emailed the person who had posted the name—Shelly Ball—a student at Brigham Young University—and my niece.

Elder Taylor wrote, "I used to visit a part-member family by the name of Ball and I was wondering if you are related to them, or know them, or know what became of them."

My niece emailed back, "I am a fourth generation Mormon in that family; my Aunt Peg knows the whole story: email her."

Imagine my surprise when I received Elder Taylor's email. As luck would have it, I remembered him. In fact, my mother and I had recently discussed him.

Back in the days when Elder Taylor was serving in the Cumorah Mission, the missionaries handed out business cards that sported full-color pictures of their home temple, as well as their mission and home addresses and phone numbers. They also handed out 5x7-inch black and white photographs of themselves. Interestingly, my mother had saved the cards and photos of all the missionaries who had called on our family over the years.

Everytime I visit my mother—who now lives in Alabama—we go through her box of old pictures. During a recent visit, we reviewed the cards and photos of the missionaries—remembering that Elder David W. Taylor of Mesa, Arizona, was one of our favorites.

So, when I received Elder Taylor's email, he was fresh on my mind. Instead of emailing him, I called information for Mesa, Arizona and asked for "David Taylor."

The operator said, "There are several of them."

I added with great confidence, "David W. Taylor".

She gave me the phone number and rang it. A man answered. "Is this Elder David W. Taylor of Mesa, Arizona, who served in the Cumorah Mission some 30 years ago?" I asked, barely able to contain my excitement.

"Yes," he replied, hesitantly—probably because it had been more than 30 years since he had been addressed as "Elder Taylor".

"This is Sis. Peg Ball Fugal, originally of New York, now of Utah, calling to report on the success of your mission."

He was so surprised to hear from me. So pleased. So anxious for news of my family.

My maternal grandmother, Lizzie Belle Kelly Rhodes, had been baptized by the LDS missionaries in south central Alabama nearly 70 years ago when she was a young mother with several children. Her two oldest children, my Uncle Walter and Aunt Nellie, were also baptized. Later, her husband and my maternal grandfather, Fate Byron Rhodes, was baptized. None of them were ever active in the church. My mother, Lee Ilar Rhodes Ball, was baptized when she was 16. She was never active either.

But the church never loses track of its members.

My parents met during the war, married within two weeks, and, after the war, moved north to Vermont, where my father had been born and raised. My two older brothers and I were born in Vermont. When I was six weeks old, my parents moved to western New York, where my father worked as the manager of a multi-dairy operation in Attica, until he bought his own dairy farm in Varysburg a dozen years later. My younger sister and brother were born in New York.

When I was a little girl returning home from elementary school, I would sometimes find the LDS missionaries visiting with my mother in the front yard.

They were almost always tall and almost always from Utah. They always wore dark suits with white shirts and ties and black nametags. They always smiled and spoke kindly to both my mother and we children.

Sometimes, we children could persuade the missionaries to follow us into the haymow, where we would swing from a rope looped over a rafter and drop into the sweet-smelling hay below. Sometimes, we could convince the missionaries to swing and drop with us—in their suits—which always made we children squeal with delight.

Sometimes, my mother would let the missionaries take we children to church with them on Sunday. She never went with us. She stayed home to cook for the missionaries. A traditional southern meal of fried chicken, mashed potatoes, milk gravy, black-eyed peas, biscuits, and pecan pie—which the missionaries loved.

Because the missionaries were my only exposure to religion, I soon began to think of myself as a Mormon. When my fourth grade teacher asked each child's religious affiliation (an act which would be considered illegal today), I proudly answered, "I'm a Mormon"—much to the shock of my teacher. Shock I did not understand.

When I shared the experience at the dinner table that evening, my father registered the same shock.

The missionary visits stopped shortly thereafter.

It was many years before I saw the missionaries again.

I was a sophomore in high school, sitting in geometry class, when the phone on the wall that connected the classroom to the front office rang. Somehow, I knew the call was for me. Sure enough, the teacher instructed me to report to the principal's office.

In those days, one was never summoned to the principal's office unless one was in trouble, or unless there was an emergency at home. I was never in trouble. I was an A-student, a former class president, a current student body officer, an award-winning orator, a member of our renowned school choir. I knew it had to be an emergency at home.

As soon as I entered the principal's office, my suspicions were confirmed by the presence of my older brother Byron and my younger sister Patti, who were sitting there weeping. The principal immediately arose from his chair, came around his desk, put his arm around my shoulders, and said with great solemnity, "Your mother has been in an accident: your father has asked me to take you children home."

In addition to milking twice daily more than five dozen cows, we also raised fowl—chickens, ducks, and turkeys. My mother loved most of all her beautiful green-headed mallard ducks.

Western New York is bordered on the north by the Great Lake Ontario, and on the west by the Great Lake Erie, and on the east by the Finger Lakes—which means every cloud that passes over western New York collects moisture from those lakes and dumps it on us. It snows nearly every day all winter: it rains nearly every day spring through fall.

That day, it had been raining hard, forming deep puddles in the main road outside our kitchen window. Mother was working at the kitchen table when she looked up and saw her precious mallards playing in the puddles in the road. "They'll get hit," she said to David, my oldest brother, who had stayed home from school that day to work on the farm, as was often required of him.

"They'll be fine," he said, moving to the window to watch the ducks. But Mother would not be deterred. She put on her rain coat and headed out the back door, around the side of the house, and out into the road, while my brother continued to watch from the window.

The rain was so heavy that neither my mother nor my brother—nor the driver of the car—could see clearly. It happened so fast that my mother never knew what hit her, the driver never knew what he had hit, and my brother could hardly comprehend what he had witnessed.

As my mother stooped to paddle the ducks out of the road, the car hit the back of her legs. She flew up over the hood of the car and smashed head first into the windshield, and then flew over the top of the car, bounced off the trunk, and crashed to the ground. The impact was so great that her shoes were later found hundreds of yards away. My brother called the rescue squad before collapsing in shock.

We children gathered at home around the round oak kitchen table and awaited news of Mother from Father who kept a constant vigil at her hospital bedside.

The top of Mother's head had been nearly scalped off, requiring more than a hundred stitches to piece it back together. Both of her arms and legs were broken. She was in a coma. There wasn't much hope for a recovery. Neighbors called and dropped in and sent cards and flowers and brought food and prayed and offered help while we waited for the inevitable.

One day, several weeks later, while my father and I were visiting my still comatose mother, two LDS missionaries appeared in the hospital room door. When I noticed them, I quivered with fear, knowing how my father felt about them. But, before Father could speak, one of the missionaries spoke to Father. "We're Mormon missionaries. Your wife is a Mormon. We understand she's had a terrible accident. We wondered if we might give her a priesthood blessing."

After my pronouncement of Mormonism at the dinner table six years earlier, my father had determined to take we children to the church of his childhood—the Methodist Church. I loved the big, old, dark building with its sweeping arches and grand organ. I joined the choir. But, when the choir director ran off with the Sunday school president, both leaving behind devastated spouses and heart-broken children, my father said, "If that's what religion does to people, then we don't need religion."

When we children became teenagers, my father decided to give religion another try. We joined the United Church of Christ, which boasted the best youth program in the county. We loved it. In fact, my two older brothers and I served youth work missions for the church in Puerto Rico. But, when my mother was hurt, and that church did not come forward to help, we left that church, too.

The missionaries were a welcome blessing in a time of great need.

From a pocket, one of the missionaries produced a small vial of what he called consecrated oil. He and his companion looked at my mother's stitched head, and decided, "We'll anoint her temples." One missionary anointed, the other pronounced the blessing.

Though we were preparing for my mother's demise, the missionary promised my mother a full recovery so she could finish raising her family.

My father and I looked at them in wonder.

Moments later, my mother awoke.

Needless to say, she made a full recovery. She finished raising her family.

My father was sufficiently humbled to invite the missionaries to resume their visits with my mother. They did so. Every single week. First, in the hospital. Later, at home. One pair of missionaries after another.

Elder Taylor was one of those missionaries.

Elder Taylor was a very handsome missionary. I remember wondering why he wasn't home, chasing girls, driving a convertible, going out for a shake and some fries, catching the latest flick, dancing the latest dance, wearing the latest fashions, going to school, working part time. I wondered why he was here, with his short hair (when long hair was the norm), in his dark suit (when no suit was the norm), preaching religion (when no religion was the norm), visiting my mother (when adults were the enemy), living by such strict rules (when no rules was the goal). It was the '60s in New York. By all counts, Elder Taylor—and all the missionaries—were geeks—who struck me as angels from heaven. I had never met anyone like them. I had never seen such countenances, never witnessed such selflessness, never felt such a spirit in young men before.

For two years, the missionaries visited my mother with no hope of activating her or baptizing her family. Still, they came. Always smiling, always offering to help, always leaving a kind word. Sometimes, they came on their preparation day and helped my father with the milking or haying. Sometimes, they played games or rode the snowmobiles with we children. Sometimes, they stayed for dinner. Always, they helped with the dishes. One summer, they helped us paint the house and barn. Always giving us the impression that we were loved—which is what eventually prompted me to investigate the church. If all those young men could love our family so much, then there must be something very right about their church.

I had wanted religion my whole life. I had figured out at a very early age that my friends who went to church were happier than those who did not—and that my friends who went to church with their families were even happier. I wanted that for myself, for my family.

I went to church with one friend after another, trying one church after another. I went to religious release time with a friend at the Baptist Church where I learned all the Bible stories. I went to mass with another friend at the Catholic Church. I went to worship services with other friends at both the Presbyterian and Episcopalian Churches. I welcomed my father's invitations to both the Methodist Church and the United Church of Christ. But something was missing. Something was not right. I was searching for the true church at the very same time that the missionaries were visiting my mother.

I made several appointments to talk to the missionaries, and then ditched them, fearing what I did not know. Often when they arrived, I would go upstairs to my bedroom, knowing they could not follow me. One day, I was sewing at the sewing machine that was situated at the base of the stairs. I did not hear the missionaries come in. They sat on the stairs, cutting off my escape route. I was forced to talk to them.

I was a bright, talented young woman—a college-bound senior in high school. I had already attended prep school on a full scholarship and I had several colleges recruiting me. I thought I knew everything. But the missionaries asked me three questions I could not answer: (1) where did you come from? (2) what are you doing here? (3) where are you going? I wanted to know the answers to those questions.

The missionaries told me the Joseph Smith story—and it made sense to me. Obviously, the church organized by Christ in his day had disappeared with the death of his last Apostle. Obviously, every church organized thereafter was the work of man. Obviously, God would return one day with his church. Obviously, he would call a prophet to do the work. It was all very logical to me.

Then the missionaries told me the Book of Mormon story—and it made sense to me. Obviously, the Israelites were the Lord's original covenant people. Obviously, when the Israelites faced destruction by the Babylonians, the Lord called a prophet to preserve his gospel and led him to a promised land. Obviously, Christ would visit those people after his resurrection and teach them his gospel. It was all very logical to me.

But logic does not convert: the Spirit does.

The missionaries encouraged me to pray.

I had never prayed in my life.

There was a window in my upstairs bedroom that reached from floor to ceiling. There was a full moon that night. Assuming that that was where God was, I knelt at the window, looked at the moon, and prayed aloud, "Heavenly Father, I don't know you, or if you are even there. But, if you are, and, if what these missionaries have taught me is true, then please tell me. And, even more importantly, tell me what to do about it."

Then something happened that I will never forget as long as I live.

The Spirit entered my body at the top of my head and flowed clear to my toes like molten gold, filling me to bursting with a confirmation of what I already knew to be true, of what I already knew I needed to do.

The missionaries baptized and confirmed me on Sunday, November 16, 1969, in the baptismal font under the Sunday school room floor in the Perry Branch building (a double-wide trailer), in Perry, New York, after the three-hour meeting block ended, with the whole branch in attendance.

And the same Spirit that filled me after my prayer filled me again after both my baptism and my confirmation.

I had found the true church.

And it ruined my life.

Little did I know how anti-Mormon people were until I told them that I was a newly baptized Mormon. Though my inactive mother was secretly proud, my father was openly displeased. My teachers turned on me—me, who had been voted Teacher's Pet every single year since kindergarten. My friends turned on me—me, their class president, their student body officer. In fact, I never went on another date for the rest of my senior year of high school. My supposedly best year of high school turned out to be my worst.

My younger sister Patti had joined the church a few months before I did. We wrote a letter to our older brother Byron who was serving in the U.S. Army in Germany and told him what we had done. He contacted the missionaries there, who baptized him.

And, then, a very strange thing happened. None of the colleges I had been applying to accepted me. Not for academic reasons, but for overcrowding reasons. It was the fall of 1969, the Viet Nam War was raging, colleges were full of student deferments: there was no room for me.

I was frantic. I had been saving money for college my whole life. I had life-long goals that would never be realized without a college education. I could not waste one more minute of my life on a farm in western New York.

The missionaries suggested BYU.

I had never heard of BYU. I didn't even know where Utah was.

I applied. BYU accepted me and sent me a scholarship. I left for BYU in September of 1970.

During my sophomore year, I met and married my husband Sherm—whose family had settled in Pleasant Grove, Utah as Mormon pioneer converts from Denmark in the late 1860s. Sherm was a returned missionary. It was the combining of a very old Mormon family with a very new Mormon family. We raised four sons in the gospel. All four served missions.

Our oldest son Jayson was one of the first missionaries called to Romania in 1991 when Romania was at first shaking off the shackles of communism. Our second son Josh served in the Brazil Sao Paulo Interlagos Mission—the smallest mission geographically in the church, but one of the most productive. Our third son Jake served in the California Carlsbad Mission—a veritable Garden of Eden mission. Our fourth son Jer served in the Korea Taejon mission, one of the toughest missions in the church.

Two of our sons have married in the temple.

My sister Patti's fiancé Gary joined the church just prior to their wedding. They were later sealed in the temple to each other and then to their four children, three of whom have served missions, one of whom has married in the temple.

My brother Byron met an LDS American school teacher named Lois in his branch in Germany. They were married in the temple and raised three daughters in the gospel, two of whom have married in the temple.

My mother, who had been inactive for nearly 50 years, finally starting going to church and eventually went to the temple.

The temple work for many of our deceased ancestors has been done.

I reported all of this to Elder Taylor.

He listened and laughed and oohed and aahed—and then he started to cry.

"What's the matter?" I asked gently, already knowing the answer.

"I never baptized a single person on my mission," he wept.

I was silent for a moment, and then I comforted, "It was not your job to baptize, Elder. It was your job to love my mother, which led to others baptizing later—baptisms that are yours because you planted the seeds."

"I thought my whole mission was a waste," he cried.

"No mission is a waste, Elder," I said. "You did exactly what the prophet asked you to do: you served a mission. You did exactly what the mission president asked you to do: you did the work, you kept the rules. You did exactly what the branch president asked you to do: you visited the less active, you visited my mother. And, with time, a miracle was wrought."

He was silent for a moment, and then I continued, "Think of the seeds of love and example and perseverance you planted in my mother's home that later took root in her children, that later led to temple marriages and children raised in the gospel, who later served missions, and baptized dozens of other people, that later led to temple work for both the living and the dead."

He was still silent.

"We can't begin to tally the harvest that began with the seeds you planted 30 years ago, Elder Taylor," I concluded, "but my best guesstimate is, it's in the hundreds, if not the thousands by now.

"I didn't know," he whispered.

"Now you do," I replied.

Then I started to cry. And we cried together. For some time. For the miracle of missionary work. For the miraculous mission of Elder David W. Taylor. And for all the other missionaries who came before and after him.

—*Peg Fugal*

⤙⤚

Samuel Smith's Important First Mission

Samuel Smith, the first missionary of the restored church, had the following interesting experience, as told by his mother:

On June 30, 1830, Samuel started on the mission to which he had been set apart by Joseph. In traveling twenty-five miles, which was his first day's journey, he stopped at a number of places in order to sell the Book of Mormon, but he was turned out as soon as he declared his principles.

When evening approached, he was faint and almost discouraged; coming to an inn that was surrounded by every appearance of plenty, he asked if the landlord would buy one of his books—a history of the origin of the Indians.

"I don't know," replied the host; "how did you get hold of it?"

"It was translated," rejoined Samuel, "by my brother, from some gold plates he found buried in the earth."

"You liar!" cried the landlord. "Get out of my house—you shan't stay one minute with your books!"

So saying, he thrust the young elder from a door of plenty.

Samuel was sick at heart, for this was the fifth time he had been turned out of doors that day.

He left the house, and traveled a short distance, then washed his feet in a small brook as a testimony against the man.

He then walked five miles further on his journey, and, seeing an apple tree a short distance from the road, he decided to spend the night beneath it.

There he lay all night, upon the cold, damp ground.

Two weeks later, when Samuel returned that way, he saw a sign on the tavern door; it read, "Smallpox".

He was informed that the innkeeper and two of his children had recently died, and that several other members of his family were ill with the malady. No other people in the village, however, had contracted the disease.

Following an arduous missionary trip that appeared to be a complete failure, Samuel returned home, carrying all his books but two. One he had given to a poor widow who had fed him, and the other he had presented to a new friend, John P. Green, a Methodist minister. After listening to Samuel's earnest testimony, he read the book prayerfully and received a conviction of its truthfulness.

Eagerly, Green carried the new volume to his brother-in-law, Phineas T. Young, who also read and believed. Phineas, in turn, presented it to his brother, Brigham Young, who read it and received a testimony of its truthfulness.

The acceptance of that sacred volume of "American scripture" started Brigham Young along the road to a famous destiny—one that was to influence greatly the history of the Church, as well as the history of western America.

This same copy of the Book of Mormon also helped convert Heber C. Kimball—and, in fewer than two years, the Greens, the Kimballs, and the Youngs, together with their households, were baptized.

Thus did Samuel, a young, unselfish servant of God, cast bread upon the waters, to find it returned a hundredfold.

—Carter E. Grant

❦

The Perfect Person

I did not come to BYU hoping to find and convert a non-member. In fact, I was surprised when I found a non-member at BYU. I assumed she was an athlete, recruited by BYU and on scholarship. She was neither. She was an investigator. She had started the discussions back home in the east. She had decided to come to BYU with another investigator friend, as well as some LDS friends.

She had been at BYU only a month when she became plagued with misgivings about the church and gospel. We met then. We talked long and hard. About the church—and everything else under the sun. Her heart began to soften and she was baptized at Thanksgiving. I spoke at her baptism.

I had never been involved in member missionary work before. Having been raised in Salt Lake, I had little opportunity. Besides, I had always been pretty opinionated about my beliefs, which does not always set well with investigators.

Just before my friend's baptism, I asked her why her conversations with me had made the difference in her decision to finally be baptized. I was surprised by her answer. "I liked your style," she said. "You were more forthright than anyone else I had ever talked to. I believed you."

There is a valuable lesson to be learned here. Everyone of us is the perfect person to tell another person about the gospel. A person who might never respond to anyone but us. That is why member missionary work is as important as serving a mission. Someone is waiting for us, for me, for you, to share the gospel with them. Someone will be baptized because my testimony, or your testimony, touched them. They are waiting for me, and you, now.

—*Ami Parker*

❧

An Illness with a Very Different Side Effect

As if surviving Y2K weren't stressful enough, shortly thereafter, I fell ill. I went to my doctor, who could not pinpoint what was wrong. Six weeks went by, with me getting sicker every week. A whole set of lab tests followed, again, to no avail. How was I to know where my strange, undiagnosed illness would lead?

When I became ill, I was serving as a Relief Society secretary. During a meeting, I learned that an inactive sister had called for a blessing for a similar condition. I did not know her, but I called her and we discussed our similar symptoms. Anything I thought might be the cause did not exist in her life, anything she thought might be the cause did not exist in my life. "It must be in the water," we laughed together.

Since I had opened the door, I was asked to be her visiting teacher.

While my friend in illness grew increasingly concerned with her deteriorating health, I remained calm, mainly because of my faith—a faith I shared with her, in hopes that it would have the same calming effect on her.

I finally realized that it was my medication that was prolonging my illness. I stopped taking it and started feeling better. Unfortunately, the same did not hold true for my friend.

I wondered why I had not discovered my problem sooner, and decided that, perhaps, my illness had been prolonged so I could better understand my friend's illness and be of comfort to her.

Comparing notes a few days later, she admitted that she had had similar thoughts. We cried and hugged.

My friend had grown less active just after high school; her husband and children were non-members. The missionaries wanted to talk to them; I suggested they wait because of her health. I was wrong: she and the children wanted to meet with the missionaries immediately. Within six weeks, two of the children were baptized, with their father present at the baptism. The grandparents and an aunt thanked me profusely for the role I played in that blessed day.

My friend and her children remain active in the church and her husband remains supportive. My friend remains ill, but less so than before.

We can't be all things to all people, but when we find a non-member or less active person with similar problems or interests, we need to reach out and offer to them the greatest gift we have to give—our testimonies of the restored church and gospel.

—Ami Parker

The Prophet David O. McKay as a Young Missionary

In 1957, our family was traveling by automobile from Glasgow to Edinburgh. We stopped in Sterling, Scotland, and father escorted us through this ancient city—his first field of missionary labor.

After showing us the magnificent castle and the house in which he lived as a young missionary, he said, "Now I want to find a certain house. It is near the foot of the castle."

We drove around and soon located it. It was an old house, with a plaque on the wall. Father told us the story.

When Father received his call to serve a mission, it came at a most inopportune time. He had just graduated from college, and had been offered a fine teaching position at Weber Academy.

He discussed it with his father, and said, "I'd like to go on a mission someday, but this just isn't the time."

His wise father replied, "It is your decision to make, David, but this is a call from the Lord."

Father reluctantly accepted.

"Then," he said, "I began tracting streets here in Sterling. The people tore up the tracts and threw them in our faces and slammed the doors on us. They cried, 'You cannae steal our lassies to take them to the walled city in Salt Lake.' They wanted no part of us, and no part of the gospel.

"I was disgusted, homesick, and discouraged. Then I came to this house and read these lines on this plaque:

> *What ere thou art, act well thy part.*

"I decided that I was here as a missionary—so I would act the part, and be a good missionary!"

—Edward R. McKay

My Best Baptism

There is a bar on every corner, or so it seems, in Sao Paulo, the world's second largest city, where I served my mission.

One night, while walking home from our labors, my companion and I passed yet another bar and a drunkard approached us.

"You're the Mormon missionaries, aren't you?" he slurred in Portuguese.

"We are," I answered boldly, pushing to get past him.

"You guys have visited me before," said the drunk.

"I don't think so," I said, growing impatient.

"Not you, but other missionaries," he said.

"Perhaps," I conceded.

"Why don't you visit me again?" he asked.

"We will, if you stop drinking," I said. "We cannot teach you if you are drinking."

We walked on, leaving the drunkard watching after us.

Some time later, when we walked by that same bar, that same drunkard was waiting for us, but this time, he was not drunk.

"I've stopped drinking," he said. "Will you come visit me now?"

Hesitant, we made an appointment with Manoel.

When we arrived, we learned that Manoel already had a Book of Mormon from the previous missionaries and had already read some of it. We gave him the first discussion, encouraged him to read 3 Nephi and Moroni's promise, and challenged him to pray about what he had learned.

When we arrived for our second visit, Manoel had read his assignment. He also had a list of questions, which we answered to his satisfaction. But, he had not prayed. He wanted our help praying. So, we prayed with him.

"I felt something," Manoel said.

"That is the Spirit," I explained.

Manoel was very excited to feel the Spirit. He liked feeling the Spirit. We talked to Manoel about recognizing and heeding the Spirit. And then we asked Manoel if he would like to be baptized.

"Yes, I want to be baptized," he answered with great determination.

Manoel also smoked. During our third visit, he announced that he had quit smoking. We introduced Manoel to the great conversion stories in Alma and set his baptism date.

I arranged for one of the District Leaders to come interview Manoel for baptism. During the interview, the District Leader asked Manoel about the Word of Wisdom. Manoel answered honestly: he had smoked that very day. The District Leader decided Manoel needed to wait for baptism.

I was afraid we had lost yet another investigator to the slave of tobacco, which enslaves many Sao Paulinos. But that was not the case with Manoel. He had felt the Spirit. Once again, he stopped smoking.

The next time we met with Manoel, who had previously been unemployed (one-third of Brazilians are unemployed), he announced that he had a new job that required him to work on the Sabbath.

"We cannot baptize someone who cannot come to church," I explained, sorry to lose him yet again.

Though most Sao Paulinos claim to be Catholic, few of them ever go to church, and most of them fail to observe the Sabbath.

The next time we met with Manoel, he announced that he had quit the job that required Sabbath work and found another. He was finally ready to be baptized. We set his baptism date.

Manoel came to the baptism clean and pressed and with his wife and children, who were members of another church—a church that was very much against the Mormons.

Manoel's marriage had suffered terribly because of his drinking. His wife thanked my companion and me for helping Manoel to stop drinking, which had greatly enhanced their marriage.

My last Sunday in the area, Manoel's wife came to church with him.

Manoel is my best baptism because he made more effort to make the necessary changes for baptism than any other person I taught on my mission.

It is not easy for any of us to make any changes.

Manoel changed because, when he first felt the Spirit, he determined right then and there that he wanted the Spirit to be with him always.

—*Josh Fugal*

❧

A Mission: A Foreordained Privilege

A recently returned mission president was visiting at the home of one of his recently released missionaries, where he met the missionary's younger brother. As he was introduced to young Fred, he asked the usual question, "How soon do you go on your mission?"

The answer was startling, but not uncommon in the LDS homes of today. Fred replied, "I don't know whether I'm going on a mission. You see, I'm in medical school and I don't want to interrupt my formal education; then, too, I'm in love with the finest girl I have met in my life and I don't want to lose her."

The mission president asked Fred if he had been formally called on a mission by the bishop. Fred answered, "Yes."

Then, the mission president used another approach and asked, "What do your parents think about your decision?" The answer was all too familiar. "They say, 'You have your free agency. It is up to you to make the decision.'"

The mission president asked Fred if he would visit with him in his office one day soon. Fred promised he would and, within a matter of days, the mission president had Fred as his visitor.

The president began their discussion by outlining to Fred the fact that his going on a mission was not hampered by the draft. He had not as yet married and truly it was his choice as to whether or not he should go. But, said the mission president, "You and your parents are in error when you say you have your free agency."

Joseph Smith writes, "Every man who has a calling to minister to the inhabitants of the world was ordained to that very purpose in the Grand Council of heaven before this world was."

The mission president continued, "It seems to me that, if we were foreordained to serve in the spirit world in the Grand Council of heaven, then we would have had to consent to that calling before being ordained. At the time we consented, we used up our free agency, and the choice was no longer ours as to whether or not we would fulfill the terms of that calling.

"In fact, it seems to me that we often misinterpret the principle of free agency in our lives. For instance, Fred, you are unmarried. You now have the privilege of going with any girl your heart chooses until you make a final determination and take her to the temple. Once you have made your choice, and she is sealed to you for the eternities, you have used up your free agency as far as girls are concerned. No longer are you able to, in any way, shop around. Your determination has been made, your free agency exercised, and no longer is free agency yours in this respect.

"By the same token, Fred, I think that when you accepted your calling in the Grand Council of heaven, to be assigned to the House of Israel, and elected to accept the call to minister to the inhabitants of the world, that your free agency, unless due to circumstances beyond your control, has been used up as far as your mission call is concerned.

"Now, you might say to yourself, 'I have no memory of having such a calling, and therefore I am not responsible to fulfill that calling.' But there is ample evidence scripturally that such callings were foreordained. Inasmuch as we walk by faith in this life, rather than by sight and remembrance, these scriptures are given to us in order that we might know of a certainty that such foreordinations are real and are a matter of record.

"For instance, in the Pearl of Great Price, Chapter 3, Verses 22-23, we read:

Now the Lord had shown unto me, Abraham, the intelligences that were organized before the world was; and among all these there were many of the noble and great ones; And God saw these souls that they were good, and he stood in the midst of them, and he said: These I will make my rulers; for he stood among those that were spirits, and he saw that they were good; and he said unto me: Abraham, thou art one of them; thou wast chosen before thou wast born.

"In the Old Testament the Lord reaffirms the practice of foreordination by revealing his word to Jeremiah as we read in Jeremiah, 1:4-5:

Then the word of the Lord came unto me, saying, Before I formed thee in the belly I knew thee; and before thou camest forth out of the womb I sanctified thee, and I ordained thee a prophet unto the nations.

"When I was 28 years old, Fred, I was ordained a Seventy by the late Levi Edgar Young, who was a member of the First Council of Seventy. After the ordination, President Young said, 'Would you like my line of authority?' After a recital of a short chain of brethren, he traced his authority back to his grand-father, Joseph Young.

"Then he repeated the circumstances connected with the calling and ordination of his grandfather to the office of Seventy. The prophet met my grandfather on the street one day and told him that it had been made known to him that my grandfather, Joseph Young, was to be the first President of the Seventy in this dispensation. In fact, the prophet said, 'You were foreordained to this very office and calling in the Grand Council of heaven before this world was and I don't know whether to reordain you or not. But, I will for the record's sake.'

"The apostles of Christ chronicle that Christ was foreordained to his calling as the redeemer of mankind. We read in 1st Peter, Chapter 1, Verses 18-20:

Forasmuch as ye know that ye were not redeemed with corruptible things, as silver and gold, from your vain conversation received by tradition from your fathers; But with the precious blood of Christ as of a lamb without blemish and without spot: Who verily was foreordained before the foundation of the world, but was manifest in these last times for you.

"Now, Fred, it is my faith and my testimony that you were called in the Grand Council of heaven to be a leavening influence to the world. In fact, to be a missionary unto our Father's other children and to gather together those who were foreordained to become members of the kingdom of Christ, and those, who in this mortal sphere, have made themselves worthy to be adopted into the House of Israel through baptism.

"Our Father in heaven has fulfilled his promises to you. You have been born in the choicest of all times when the light of the gospel is on the earth. You live under the direction of a living prophet. You have choice parentage and you have been born under the covenant. You have been assigned to the House of Israel. The only way you can show your appreciation to your Father in heaven for these great blessings, which exceed all other blessings in this life, is to accept your mission call and be of service in our Father's eternal plan. You have even specifically been assigned to the House of Ephriam, which is the tribe of service.

"The Lord rarely speaks of the children of Ephriam but what he refers to them as, 'my servants', as is evidenced in the 133rd section of the Doctrine and Covenants, where the Lord is telling of the gathering in the last days in the center place of Zion:

> *And they shall bring forth their rich treasures unto the children of Ephriam, My servants. And the boundaries of the everlasting hills shall tremble at their presence. And there shall they fall down and be crowned with glory, even in Zion, by the hands of the servants of the Lord, even the children of Ephriam.*

"In chapter 12 of Revelations, written by John, the Lord describes in detail to us the battle that took place in heaven. Many of us think that when Satan and his angels were cast out of heaven that the battle ended. However, the battle ground merely changed places and John records a warning to those who live on the earth in verse 12:

> *Woe to the inhabiters of the earth and of the sea! For the Devil is come down unto you, having great wrath, because he knoweth that he hath but a short time.*

"Joseph Smith records in his writings, 'In relation to the kingdom of God, the Devil always sets up his kingdom at the very same time in opposition to God.'

"Now, Fred," concluded the mission president, "let me put it to you cold turkey. Are you going to fulfill your promises to the Lord, or are you going to find an excuse and follow the enticings of the evil one, who, in the battle in heaven, drew away with him one third of the children of our Father in heaven?"

There was a long pause as the mission president waited for an answer. Then came the firm resolution, "I'm going to talk to my bishop and tell him that, if he will reissue my call, then I will fulfill my foreordained privilege."

The rightness of his decision was evidenced one year later when Fred wrote to his concerned advisor:

> *Dear President, I first must thank you for your inspired and persuasive remarks during my indecisive moments of one year past. Having now completed one year of my mission, I can now gaze in retrospect and classify this as the most developing year of my life. I wrote Mom and Dad recently and told them that, if ever I influence a younger generation, I would hope to instill within them the vital importance of each young man fulfilling an honorable mission. I sometimes could weep as I think how nearly I overlooked the only value of lasting import in my life—the gospel.*
> —David A. McDougal

✢

The Greatest Decision I Ever Made

Great-uncle Benjamin had died more than 30 years ago, and some of his belongings were packed away in old trunks in the farmhouse attic.

"I wonder why Grandpa saved all this stuff all these years," John grumbled, as he helped sort through it with his mother and sister.

Grandpa had died a few weeks before, and Jennie Lynn, his only surviving daughter, and her two children had come to clean out the old family home.

John threw a shapeless felt hat into a large barrel in the center of the room. "Man, do you ever wonder if your family tree has blight attacking its roots?" he said. "I mean, what in the world would they want to save all this junk for? Look at this old dilapidated book for instance: Pamela, or Virtue Rewarded. Brother!"

"That," replied his sister Alice with great indignation, "is a copy of the first English novel ever written. Kindly place it carefully in the save box."

"Well, what about this? John asked. "A partially used notebook? Who in their right mind would save that?"

Jennie walked over and looked at the book.

"Can you make out what it says?" Alice asked.

"Easy," John replied, as he sat down and started to read, skipping pages here and there.

May 4, 1888: Mother locked my violin in the cedar chest again this morning She said it's too big a temptation for me before the cows are milked. She's right I suppose. It's a good thing the other boys are more diligent than I or we'd never be able to feed all eight of us from these few acres. If Father were still alive we'd manage better.

September 3, 1888: Mr. Carter told Mother today that he has taught me all he knows, and I need a more advanced teacher. There is a Sis. Kendall over in Coalville who is supposed to have played at one time with the Philadelphia orchestra before joining the church and moving west. Mother promised I could ask her if she would take me as a pupil. The only trouble is going to be how much she will charge for lessons. I am to be allowed to take charge of the chickens and keep the egg money to pay for my music

April 8, 1892: I realized today that there are three things I love better than all else: the Lord, my family, and my music. And, I know now, that the love of one thing does not necessarily preclude the love of another. When they're all good things, they all go together.

December 1, 1892: It's terribly late, but I can't sleep. I've been copying music all evening with Mother's help. I've been asked to travel to Salt Lake to audition for a place with the territorial orchestra…

March 5, 1893: After several weeks of practicing, interspersed with hours of prayer, I went to Salt Lake and auditioned. Mr. Dean, the conductor, told me I was the most accomplished violinist he had heard west of Denver. There probably aren't too many west of Denver that he has heard, but Mother was pleased when I told her. I am to be in Denver rehearsals early in the fall, and I'll be earning enough to keep myself, plus a little to spare for Mother and the others. Sunday, in sacrament meeting, I'm to play the Mozart selection I learned for the tryouts.

March 11, 1893: Why has this happened now? Why, just at this point in my life? After sacrament meeting on Sunday, Bishop Reynolds called me into his office, and asked me how the tryouts had gone. I told him that I had been hired, and he asked me if I couldn't put off playing with the orchestra for a couple of years. He explained to me that, before I start earning money, there is something else I owe the Lord. With no doubt in his mind that it is the will of the Lord, he asked me to accept a mission call. I know I owe everything I have to my God, and a couple of years away from my violin shouldn't be too much to ask, but I think it's giving up almost more than I can bear. Still, I knew the uncertainty in my own heart was more dread than doubt, so I promised the bishop that if there was any way for us to raise the money, I would accept the call.

March 13, 1893: Last night, I told Mother about the mission call. She was overjoyed. Father had always wanted to serve a mission, she said, but he had been killed before he was able. Now, I could fill a mission in his place. When I asked her how we were going to raise the money, her face clouded. Explaining to her that I would not allow her to sell any more of the land, I told her of the conditional promise that I had given the bishop. She looked at me quietly for a moment and then she said, "Ben, there is a way we can raise the money. This family owns one thing that is of great enough value to finance your mission. Your violin."

March 17, 1893: The promise must be kept, and there is a way. Next Monday, I will go to Salt Lake and sell my violin. If I am able to raise the needed sum for my passage, I will leave immediately on my mission. I have made my decision and I am at peace.

March 23, 1893: I awoke this morning and took my violin from its case. All day long I played the music I love. In the evening, when the light grew dim and I could see no longer, I placed the instrument in its case. It will be enough. Tomorrow, I leave.

"That's it," John whispered. "It ends there. What happened? Did he come back and get another violin? Did he get his job back after his mission?"

"I don't know," Jennie replied. "I suppose there's somebody around who does, but I don't really mind having the story end there. You already know the most important thing about him."

"Wait!" yelped John. "Look, there's a little more writing at the back of the notebook." He glanced at the short entry, coughed a little to cover the other sound that had almost escaped his throat, and handed the book to Jennie. "You read it, Mom," he said.

Jennie took the book, moved closer to the small gabled window to catch the fading light, and looked at the page. The hand that wrote these words was not quite as steady or as firm as the one that had started the journal, but the letters were still carefully and evenly formed. She read:

June 23, 1938: The greatest decision I ever made in my life was to give up something I dearly loved to the God I loved even more. He has never forgotten me for it.
                                                                          —Benjamin Landart

❧

We Love Each Other

A lonely young Persian student was in Munich, struggling to find meaning to life, but deeply disturbed by the materialism and selfishness that seemed to fill post-war Europe.

He heard a knock at the door one day, and two humble LDS missionaries stood before him. He was not the least bit interested in religion. In fact, cynicism and doubt had filled his soul until he was nearly persuaded that there was no God or any real meaning to life. The only thing that interested him about these two young men was their English—he had mastered four languages, but English was not one of them.

He invited them in, but, as they began their discussion, he cautioned, "I don't want to hear about your God or your religion. I only want to know one thing: what do you people do for one another?"

He waited, and a look of doubt crossed his dark features as the elders exchanged glances. Finally, the spokesman for the two said, softly, "We love one another."

Nothing he could have said would have been more electrifying than this simple utterance, for the Holy Ghost immediately bore witness to his soul that these missionaries were true servants of the Lord.

Shortly thereafter, he was baptized, moved to America, and began studying for his doctorate—all because a young missionary declared a simple truth.

—Russ Price

❧

What Kind of Missionaries Will We Be?

Two men once sat in an airplane. They began to talk. The one asked the other what he did for a living. The second man answered that he was a LDS missionary. The first man commented that he didn't have much use for missionaries—or others who went around trying to get people to change their minds.

The missionary stated that the other man was also a missionary. The man emphatically denied it, and asked how the missionary could say such a thing.

The missionary replied that everything the man did and said influenced others in one way or another, so he was a missionary for his way of life.

Many members of the church have said that they would do anything they were called to do in the church, except be a missionary.

But you are a missionary!

Those who keep high moral standards, treat the members of their families and their neighbors according to the gospel of Jesus Christ, pay a full tithing, obey the word of wisdom, attend their meetings, and read the scriptures regularly are all missionaries.

Obviously, those who do not do these things are also missionaries.

We must understand that life is one great full-time mission with people constantly watching how we act, what we say, and what we do. In simple terms, a mission is living with a purpose—be it for good or for bad.

President McKay said, "Every member a missionary". That statement holds as true today as it did when he said it. We are all missionaries! It is not a question of whether or not we want to be missionaries. That has been decided. The only question is: What kind of missionaries will we be?

—Bishopric Message, Kaysville, Utah 10th
Ward Newsletter, June 2, 1996

❧

You Were That Man!

I am a teacher at the Ogden LDS Institute of Religion, and have been since 1967 when I was transferred from Southern California.

Recently, I received a telephone call.

"My name is Steven Stone. Are you the Johansen who had a baby girl born on March 19, 1967, in the Westminster Hospital in California?"

"No, we didn't have a baby girl born on that date, but we did have a baby boy born that date in that hospital," I replied.

"Do you remember talking to me about the LDS Church in the father's waiting room while our wives were in the delivery room at the same time?" the caller continued.

"I do indeed remember that conversation. I was a Seventy in the Garden Grove Ward in California, and it was the era of the 'golden question'. I tried it on you while we were both alone in the father's waiting room. 'What do you know about the Mormon Church? Would you like to know more?' You showed an interest, and I got your name and address for the missionaries. I was so excited that when I was invited in to hold my wife's hand during the last stages of labor, that's all I could talk about!

"You were that man! You must have joined the Church!" I said excitedly.

"Yes, I did. And, so did my wife and our four children," he replied. "We had the missionaries come shortly after my wife came home from the hospital, and we were baptized that same year—in 1967. I have been looking for you all these years to thank you for sharing the gospel with me. I knew only that your last name was Johansen, and I have been calling on all the Johansens I can find, in search of you. I found your name on a brochure sent out by the Institute to our college-aged daughter."

There was a lump in my throat and tears in my eyes as I said, "I remember that incident, but I didn't remember your name."

He added, "That's because I didn't change your life: you changed mine!"

You often wonder what happens to the people with whom you try to share the gospel in your conversations. After 27 years, I found out!

—*Jerald R. Johansen, LDS Church News*

Why Bother?!

I was very angry with my mother. And had been for years.

Her mother, father, oldest brother, and oldest sister had all been baptized by the LDS missionaries in south central Alabama when she was a baby.

Her life had been spared by a missionary priesthood blessing when she contracted bone cancer as a little girl.

She had been baptized at the age of 16 by the missionaries.

Though the missionaries visited regularly, neither she nor her family were ever active in the church.

When she married my father and moved to Vermont, the missionaries found her there, and visited regularly.

Still, she remained inactive.

When our family moved to western New York, the missionaries found her there, and visited regularly.

Still, she remained inactive.

A tragic automobile accident left her dying when she was a middle-aged mother with five teenaged children.

Once again, her life was spared by a missionary priesthood blessing.

The missionaries visited weekly during her recuperation.

Still, she remained inactive.

Prompted by the visits of the missionaries, three of her five children finally listened to the discussions and were baptized. I was one of them.

We all married in the church: one in the temple, the other two later sealed.

We all raised families in the church.

Then my father died.

It was he who had discouraged mother's church activity. Now that he was gone, she was free to go to church without repudiation.

Still, she remained inactive.

And then she moved back home to Alabama.

Meanwhile, grandchildren started departing on missions.

Still, she remained inactive.

Always claiming she was a Mormon, while scorning the Word of Wisdom.

Then Mother had a heart attack—her third near-death experience.

Once again, she was spared by a missionary priesthood blessing.

Shortly thereafter, she called and asked me if I could help her catch up her tithing.

"Tithing?" I shrieked. "You don't even go to church!"

Come to find out, she did.

Once she had left New York, and re-established herself in the hometown of her childhood, she started going to the little tiny branch there.

The building was so small that it resembled a doll house.

Only 40 of the 150 members were active.

But they were stalwarts.

When Mother went back to church, she also began addressing her Word of Wisdom problems.

She was paying tithing on her social security income, and on the money we children sent to her.

She had home teachers and visiting teachers.

She occasionally went visiting teaching herself.

She even taught a Relief Society lesson every now and then.

Her bishop was a fine young man, whose wife and children were not members. He paid special attention to Mother.

Her home teachers and visiting teachers spoke to her at church every Sunday and checked on her at home once a month, making sure she was invited and had a ride to every church function.

The missionaries assigned to her branch mowed her lawn on their preparation days.

"Why the sudden interest in tithing?" I asked, not without a little contempt.

"I'm getting ready to go to the temple," she said.

I was speechless.

I had figured that I would do my parents' temple work after they died. I had never counted on going to the temple with either one of them while they were still alive.

I called my LDS brother and sister. We decided to take Mother to the Toronto Temple, which was the temple district in which she had once lived, and in which my brother and sister still lived, in New York.

I flew out from Utah where I lived, with my genealogy work in tow. I put up all four of our families at the Marriott nearest the temple. The children played at the hotel while we adults went to the temple.

I handed my genealogy to a temple worker. She asked if we wanted to do the work for the dead ancestors listed while we were in the temple that day. We did.

When we left, 28 ordinances for both our living and dead family had been completed.

It was one of the greatest days of my life.

I had been angry with my mother for years. For having the gospel and never living it. For refusing to embrace it, miracle after miracle. For refusing to embrace it, even when her children did, even when her grandchildren did.

And, I wondered repeatedly why God bothered to continue to spare her life with missionary priesthood blessings—first, the bone cancer; then, the car accident; then, the heart attack—only to have her make a mockery of him.

One day, watching my mother with our family, the answer came to me.

God spared her from bone cancer so she could grow up and marry and have we children.

Then, he spared her from accidental death so we children would listen to the missionaries and join the church.

Then, he spared her from death by a heart attack so she herself could become converted and go to the temple and be sealed to her family.

We cannot always see or understand the ways of God, but we can certainly trust them, especially when it comes to our families.

—*Peg Fugal*

The Baptisms I Missed

The horror of every missionary's life is to find and prepare someone for baptism only to be transferred prior to the baptism. That happened to me three times on my mission.

The Adams family

I was a brand new missionary with my first companion in my first area—nervous, unsure, overwhelmed. In that area was a lone-member family, named Adams. The mother was a member, the father was not; there were three children: a 16-year-old and twin 11-year-olds.

The previous sister missionaries had been working with the Adams family for almost a year—whose interest in the church had began with a son and daughter-in-law who had joined the church. My companion and I were to continue the work. I was so fearful of failing, of undoing all the hard work that had proceeded me. But that was not the case.

The Adams family immediately embraced me, made me feel welcome, made me realize why I was serving a mission, and gave me confidence to teach and bear testimony. The mom seemed my mother away from home; the 16-year-old, the little sister I never had. We spent many productive hours teaching the gospel and talking. It was the best possible start to a mission that I could ever have hoped for.

Then I was transferred. I was devastated. Not only had I lost the chance to follow my work through to baptism, but I had lost my anchor.

Later, while serving in another area, I received news that the 16-year-old had been baptized.

Still later, while serving in yet another area, I received news that the father had been baptized.

Two baptisms that should have been mine, credited to someone else.

I could have been angry.

I was not.

I was just glad to be part of the process.

Gladness that was later rewarded.

While I was serving in still another area, one of the two sister missionaries working with the Adams family had to return home for some emergency dental work. My companion and I were assigned to assist the lone missionary, who was preparing the 11-year-old Adams twins for baptism.

My companion and I joined the discussions, helped prepare for the baptism, and attended the baptism—where we watched the newly baptized Adams father baptize his twins. It was the greatest day of my mission.

Carol

While serving in Monterey, California, my companion and I were meeting with an investigator named Carol, whose introduction to the church could be chalked up to mechanical problems.

Carol, who lived in California, and her husband, who lived in Alaska, were flying between the two once, with a stopover in Salt Lake City, where they wanted to visit Temple Square, which time did not allow.

Several years later, Carol, alone this time, was flying between Alaska and California again. When she arrived at the airport, she learned that her plane had mechanical problems, and that she had been put on another flight with another lay-over in Salt Lake City. This time, Carol had time to visit Temple Square.

Carol loved Temple Square and the sister missionaries who gave her the tour. She was impressed enough to ask for a copy of the Book of Mormon and for the missionaries to call on her.

First, the elders contacted her, then we sister missionaries took over. We weren't sure how far along Carol was in her studies or testimony, so we started all over again.

Carol was having a hard time giving up coffee. We taught her the quit-smoking program, but, instead, called it the quit-coffee program.

During her travels around the country, Carol always visited other wards and stakes, and was always impressed that, no matter where she went, the church was always the same.

Still, Carol was not ready to commit to baptism—mainly because her husband was opposed.

One time, when Carol's husband was visiting from Alaska, we left some fresh cinnamon buns and juice outside their door early one morning—which warmed his attitude toward us considerably.

As luck would have it, the week I was due to be transferred, Carol committed to baptism—which took place after I departed.

Once again, I could have been angry; instead, I was happy to be part of the process. My happiness was rewarded with a continued friendship with Carol through the mail.

—Darcy Somerhalder

❧

Love Thy Companion

One of the great tests of missionary life is learning to live with and love our companions, many of whom are nearly impossible to live with and even more impossible to love. Such is said to be good training for marriage.

When my companion and I reached Santa Cruz, we were new to each other and the area—which had not had sister missionaries for some time.

The ward, who had always had and, hence, preferred, elders, took a long time getting used to we sister missionaries—which hurt a little. Okay, a lot.

The area, which was somewhat dangerous, was better suited to elders tracting than to sisters tracting. We were hesitant, if not down-right scared, most of the time.

It was only my second area, Sis. Seeley was only my second companion, I had left behind in my previous area a family who loved me like a daughter and who were preparing for baptism: I was miserable. In fact, if I had ever wanted to leave the mission field, it was in Santa Cruz. And my companion knew it.

Now, some companions would respond to a companion like me with great disdain, arguing with the discouraged missionary, ordering her around, calling her to repentance, reporting her to the mission president, going on splits to avoid her. Such was not the case with Sis. Seeley.

Instead, she followed the admonition of the Savior, and showed forth an even greater issue of love.

As often happens with down-trodden missionaries, I got sick—the bane of every companion's existence—except Sis. Seeley. She immediately rallied the other missionaries for fasts and prayers, the elders for blessings, the ward members for food. She went on splits—not to get away from me, but to give me a variety of company while I recovered. Meanwhile, she remained positive and anxiously engaged in the work of that area.

Thanks to Sis. Seeley's love, I regained my strength and commitment, and together we found a lovely family to teach. Once again, I was transferred before the baptism took place. But, thanks to Sis. Seely's guiding hand, I was there to take part in the process.

—Darcy Somerhalder

❧

The Marks of a Man

As I jumped on board my flight from Miami to Salt Lake City, I paused for a moment to catch my breath.

Seated near the front of the plane was an excited young man, probably 19, sitting with his parents. His hair was short, his clothes new and sharp. His suit was fitted perfectly, his black shoes still retained that store-bought shine. His body was in good shape, his face and hands were clean. In his eyes, I could see a nervous look, his movements were that of an actor on opening night.

He was obviously flying to Utah to become a missionary for the LDS Church. I smiled as I walked by, and took pride in belonging to the same church where these young men and women voluntarily serve the Savior for two years. With this special feeling, I continued back to where my seat was located.

As I sat down in my seat, I looked to the right and, to my surprise, saw another missionary, sleeping in the window seat. His hair was also short, but that was the only similarity between the two.

This one was obviously returning home, and I could tell at a glance what type of missionary he had been.

The fact that he was already asleep told me a lot. His entire body seemed to let out a big sigh. It looked as if this was the first time in two years that he had even slept, and I wouldn't be surprised if it was.

As I looked at his face, I could see the heavy bags under his eyes, the chapped lips, and the scarred and sunburned face caused by the fierce Florida sun.

His suit was tattered and worn. A few of the seams were coming apart, and I noticed that there were a couple of tears that had been hand-sewn with a very sloppy stitch.

I saw the nametag, crooked, scratched, and bearing the name of the church he represented, the engraving of which was almost all worn away.

I saw the knee of his pants, worn and white, the result of many hours of humble prayer.

A tear came to my eye as I saw the things that really told me what kind of missionary he had been.

I saw the marks that made this boy a man.

His feet, the two that had carried him from house to house, now lay there swollen and tired. They were covered by a pair of worn-out shoes. Many of the large scrapes and gouges had been filled in by countless polishings.

The books, lying across his lap, were his scriptures—the word of God. Once new, these books, which testify of Jesus Christ and his mission, were now torn, bent, and ragged from use.

His hands, those big, strong hands which had been used to bless and teach, were now scarred and cut from knocking on doors.

Those were indeed the marks of a man.

And, as I looked at him, I saw the marks of another man, the Savior, as he was hanging on the cross for the sins of the world.

His feet, those that had once carried him throughout the land during his ministry, were now nailed to the cross.

His side, now pierced with a spear, sealing his testimony with his life.

His hands, the hands that had been used to ordain his servants and bless the sick, were also scarred with the nails that were pounded to hang him on the cross.

Those were the marks of that great man.

As my mind returned to the missionary, my whole body seemed to swell with pride and joy because I knew, by looking at him, that he had served his Master well.

My joy was so great that I felt like running to the front of the plane, grabbing the new missionary, and bringing him back to see what he could become, what he could do.

But, would he see the things I saw? Could anyone? Or, would he see just the outward appearance of that mighty elder, tired and worn-out, almost dead?

As we landed, I reached over and tapped the returning missionary to wake him up.

As he awoke, it seemed like new life poured into his body. His whole frame seemed to fill as he stood up, tall and proud. As he turned his face toward mine, I saw a light that I had never seen before.

I looked into his eyes. Those eyes. I will never forget those eyes. They were the eyes of a prophet, a leader, a follower, a servant. They were the eyes of the Savior.

No words were spoken. No words were needed.

As we disembarked, I stepped aside to let him go first. I watched as he walked, slow but steady, tired but strong. I followed him, and found myself walking the way he did.

When I came through the doors, I saw the returning missionary in the arms of his parents, and I couldn't hold it any longer. With tears streaming down my face, I watched these loving parents greet their son, who had been away for a such a long time, and I wondered if our parents in heaven would greet us in the same manner.

Will they wrap their arms around us and welcome us home from our journey on earth? I believe they will. I just hope that I will be worthy enough to receive such praise, as I'm sure this missionary will.

I said a silent prayer, thanking the Lord for missionaries like this young man. I don't think I will ever forget the joy and happiness he brought to me that day.

Well done, thou good and faithful servant!

—*David Bryan Viser*

Elder Buckley

Though the missionaries had been visiting our family off and on for many years, it was Elder Buckley who finally caught my attention.

Elder Buckley was a little different from the other missionaries. For one thing, he was quite tall, taller by several inches than we New Yorkers. For another, he had big ears that stuck out, but only added to his charm, along with his ever-present smile, and his quirky personality. For instance, he had a silly habit of walking right up to you and sticking his finger in your ear to get you to listen to him. I did.

It was Elder Buckley who persuaded me to pray about what he had taught me.

It was Elder Buckley who baptized me.

My father did not like the missionaries or want anything to do with the church. He liked Elder Buckley because Elder Buckley liked him. Talked to him, helped him, loved him, never pressured him.

It was Elder Buckley who suggested I attend BYU.

It was Elder Buckley who picked me up at the airport, gave me my first tour of the church sites in Salt Lake City, and delivered me to BYU.

It was Elder Buckley who took me home to his family my first Thanksgiving away from home, and drove me to the airport my first Christmas back home.

When Elder Buckley married and took his wife to visit his mission, they stopped to visit my parents. My father was so happy to see the only missionary he ever liked.

It was Elder Buckley who attended my wedding, and the baptism of my second son, and the farewell of my first son.

It was Elder Buckley I called when my first son visited my oldest brother, who was both a Catholic and an anti-Mormon, and who kept my son up all night harrassing and haranguing him about the church. I was so upset.

"Do you know what I think happened?" Elder Buckley calmly asked. "I think that was the first time the Spirit had been in your brother's home and it frightened him." I was immediately comforted and intrigued.

It was Elder Buckley who sent a Christmas card and letter and picture every year in an effort to stay in touch.

It was Elder Buckley I called when my mother, who had been baptized at 16, but never active until 62, decided to go to the temple. I was weeping with both shock and joy.

"Do you know what I think?" Elder Buckley ventured. "I think your dad got over on the other side, decided we were right, and wanted his family; so, he is prompting your mom to go to the temple to be sealed to him and to seal their babies to them." I wept for hours contemplating that thought and our joyous reunion as an eternal family one day.

It was Elder Buckley who I turned to when one of my sons was refusing to serve a mission. "The Spirit will speak to him," Elder Buckley assured me. It did. And my son served a mission.

Elder Buckley taught me the gospel and baptized me. But, like all missionaries and their converts, his influence did not stop there. Elder Buckley has remained my missionary, influencing my life for good, for my entire 32 years in the church. I thank Heavenly Father every night in my prayers for sending Elder Buckley to me and my family.

—Peg Fugal

Thousands of Prayers

Toward the end of my mission, I was feeling extremely physically worn out and tired. Each morning, as I awoke and took the first few steps of the day, pain would shoot up my feet and legs. I dragged myself through each day, collapsing into bed at night, exhausted. I wondered how my worn-out body could walk another five feet, let alone five or more miles each day.

At that time, I had the opportunity to go to the temple. There, I received not only spiritual uplift, but a physical boost as well. It happened during the endowment prayer.

As usual, the officiator blessed the missionaries. But it wasn't the usual quick and simple reference to the missionaries; instead, it was a detailed and specific physical blessing. He blessed the missionaries' feet, their legs, their arms, their shoulders, and so on, through the entire body. As he said this prayer, I felt strength returning to my limbs.

As I left the temple that day, I felt as fresh as if it were my first day in the mission field. That physical "high" stayed with me for several days and would return again and again whenever I remembered that prayer.

The more I pondered the prayer, the more I realized that every temple endowment prayer includes a blessing for the missionaries. That's hundreds of prayers by thousands of people everyday. Add to that all the personal prayers of the members blessing the missionaries. That's a lot of power and strength being sent our way!

Every time I was ready to drop and give up, I would focus my thoughts on all those prayers and receive a refueling of both body and spirit. That's what got me through the final months of my mission.

—Renee Rhoton

Fishing to Fill Our Teaching Pool

One day, my companion and I had been tracting for nine hours straight with no luck. We went home and, the next morning, we started all over again.

We tracked for four hours straight this time and found only one half-hearted contact.

We were about to leave the area, when we decided to try one more street—praying the whole time that we might find someone to teach because our teaching pool was empty.

We were prompted to go to the opposite end of the area where we had been tracting, and to knock on the door of the second house. Inside, we found a family of five who were interested in learning more.

When we left the family, we started knocking again, but to no avail.

For some reason, we were prompted to go fishing (which was allowed in our mission).

We were fishing in our suits and ties for only five minutes before we had five more people interested in taking a Book of Mormon and learning more.

We now had a total of ten people in our previously empty teaching pool.

It was through diligence and perserverence that the Lord blessed us to find these people.

—*Tony Rhoton*

❧

My Father Car-Pooled with an LDS Man

My father used to car-pool with an LDS man who worked at the same high school where my father taught. Over the years, my father and this man became friends. My younger brothers and I were in elementary school at the time; our mother was an alcoholic.

One day, the LDS man asked my father if he would like to learn more about the LDS Church. My father said he would, so the man sent the LDS missionaries to visit us.

My mother was not very happy about the missionaries' visit; she told father and the missionaries to go outside and talk on the patio.

When the missionaries left, they left a copy of *The Friend* for we children to read; I read every story to my brothers.

They left our father a copy of the Book of Mormon.

Father began reading the Book of Mormon at night in bed, leaving it on his bedside table during the day, where my mother found it and also read it—in a week!

When the missionaries returned, my mother told them that she knew the Book of Mormon was true. She said she was ready to accept the challenge of Moroni and wanted to hear the discussions—inside the house. When my mother learned the Word of Wisdom, she stopped drinking.

Two months later, my mother, my father, and I were baptized. My two brothers were later baptized.

That was almost 40 years ago.

My brothers both served missions, and all three of we children married in the temple; three of my sons have also served missions.

It is hard to imagine the lives that have been touched by my brothers and my sons, serving as missionaries all over the world—all because my father once car-pooled with an LDS man who was not afraid to talk about his religion.

—*Jill Cate*

❧

These Guajiros

I used to imagine that my most memorable missionary experiences would be the dramatic or miraculous ones. Not necessarily so. Upon returning from my mission to Venezuela six years ago, I discovered that the quieter, more humble experiences were the ones I remembered most.

In one area of Maracaibo lives a wonderful family of Guajiros (Indians). The family is large and the surroundings are cramped and dirty but, typical of South American people, they are a cheerful lot.

The family owns a bus. The father's occupation is driving bus. The family bus is affectionately called Moroni. (There is also a son named Nefi.)

The family bus often makes runs to transport ward members to various church meetings, firesides, activities, etc.

This special family introduced we sister missionaries to another special family—the Martinezes—a mother with four daughters, who embraced the gospel and were baptized.

Through their humility and dedicated service to others, these Guajiros show their love and enthusiasm for the gospel of Jesus Christ. And, surprisingly, that is what I remember most from my missionary experience in Venezuela.

—Megan Gladwell

❧

The Power of Testimony

I grew up in the church and did all the things one is supposed to do—except read the Bible and Book of Mormon all the way through. So, when my mission call to the Bible belt of North Carolina arrived, I felt totally unprepared and inadequate.

Sure enough, everyone my trainer and I tracted had a solid understanding of the Bible. I was doomed. Then I learned perhaps the most important lesson of my mission. "It is the Spirit that converts," counseled my trainer, "not what you do or don't know."

About three months into my mission, I was called to serve as a senior companion, training a brand new missionary. Again, I felt totally unprepared and inadequate. I prayed that my new companion had a good understanding of the scriptures.

Not only did my new companion not have a good understanding of the scriptures, but he also he didn't even want to be on a mission; in fact, he wasn't even sure he had a testimony. The sole reason he was serving a mission was because his girlfriend would not marry him until he did. My prayers were not answered.

At that time, my new companion and I were teaching a young family with three small children who were nearing baptism.

As we were leaving our apartment one evening to teach this family one of the last discussions, our phone rang. It was the mother of our family, wanting to know if her minister could sit in on our discussion.

This family was very active in their own church—and I'm sure their minister did not want to lose them. Not knowing any better, I welcomed the minister's presence.

That was the longest bike ride of my life. I worried myself sick all the way to the house of our family.

When we arrived, I was very relieved to find that the minister was not there. Unfortunately, he arrived a short time later—loaded down with a large stack of books and a tape recorder.

After the introductions, we asked if we could begin with prayer. I don't remember who said the prayer, but I do remember saying my own silent prayer and pleading with the Lord to be with us.

After the prayer, the minister immediately took the lead and proceeded to teach us from the scriptures and books he had brought. Then, he played a tape from previous members who had since been "saved"—"saved", presumably, from the Mormons.

The longer the minister talked, the more worried I became. He was so convincing that I almost believed him! And, if he was persuading me, then surely he was persuading my comp and our family.

By the time the minister had completed his presentation, my testimony had fallen asleep. Had he challenged me to baptism, I might have accepted.

I was devastated.

Not knowing what to do, I excused myself and went to the bathroom. I remember sitting on the edge of the bathtub, wondering what to do. I got down on my knees and asked the Lord for help. I had never prayed like I did at that moment.

I immediately heard a voice telling me to bear my testimony. I remember thinking: oh, great—my testimony is napping!

As I wrestled with that idea, I again heard the voice telling me to bear my testimony.

Again, I wondered what good that would do. My testimony was snoozing, my companion wasn't sure he had a testimony, and our investigating family's testimony was merely a seed that had yet to germinate.

A third time I heard the voice: bear your testimony.

This time I obeyed.

I returned to the room, looked the minister straight in the eye, and bore my testimony.

I told him that I knew Joseph Smith was a prophet of God and that he did in reality see and speak with God the Father and his son Jesus Christ. I told him that I knew the Book of Mormon was the word of God and that it was translated by the gift and power of God...

I don't remember everything I said, but I do remember thinking to myself, "I don't really know these things."

As I bore testimony, the Spirit grew stronger and stronger—and, before long, I did know—deep down inside.

When I finished, a wonderful thing happened. My companion, for the first time in his life, bore his testimony.

When he finished, our investigating family, one by one, bore their testimonies.

And, I just sat there and watched the miracle unfold.

The Spirit was so strong that, when everyone finished, the minister got up, gathered his materials, and left.

We all sat there for a moment and then we all stood up and hugged each other.

That was the birth of my testimony—and the testimonies of each and every one in that room. We were all spiritually converted at that very moment—and our investigating family was baptized.

Never again did I worry about my knowledge or ability throughout the remainder of my mission. I now had a testimony of the gospel. I had personally witnessed what my trainer had tried to teach me from the beginning—it is the the Spirit that converts.

There is a great power in bearing testimony.

To this day, I thank Heavenly Father for that experience that changed so many lives.

Never will I doubt again.

—*Steve Wernli*

✌

Their Long Wait Over

Some of our best investigators are right under our noses and we don't even know it. I found this to be literally true while serving in the mission office.

The mission staff had resided in an upstairs apartment of a duplex for many years. While I was living there, two school teachers were living downstairs.

Though we always spoke to the teachers in our comings and goings, we had never approached them.

One preparation day, I was getting something out of the car while one of the school teachers, Helen, was washing her car. She asked who we were and what we did.

I told her we were missionaries for the Church of Jesus Christ of Latter-day Saints. Then, I was prompted to ask her the golden question, "Would you like to know more?"

To my surprise, Helen was very interested in learning more, so we set up an appointment for that evening.

We taught Helen the first discussion, and she was so receptive that she could hardly wait to learn more. She invited us to return the next evening. We taught her the second discussion, and asked if she wanted to be baptized. Not only did she want to be baptized, but she wanted to know how soon we could do it!

We invited Helen to a baptism at the church on Friday, and encouraged her to come to church with us at least once before her own baptism. Every night between then and the Friday baptism, we taught her another discussion.

The Spirit at the Friday baptism was very strong; Helen felt it and begged to be baptized that very evening. Again, we encouraged her to come to church first.

We taught the final discussion Saturday night and Helen joined us for church on Sunday. Things could not have gone better. She loved the meetings and classes and people and immediately started making new friends.

After church, we made an appointment to discuss her baptism.

When we reached Helen's apartment, we knocked and knocked and knocked, but she did not come to the door for some time. When she did, she stuck her head out the door and said, "I cannot talk to you", and closed the door.

My companion and I stood there staring at the door, wondering what had gone wrong when everything had gone so right. Many too right, maybe too fast, we thought.

We returned to our apartment to contemplate the situation, surmising it was Satan, who often troubles investigators.

An hour later, there was a knock on our door. It was Helen. "Come downstairs," she said, "we need to talk."

Shortly after Helen had returned home from church on Sunday, she knelt in prayer. Helen's grandmother—to whom she had been very close, and who had been dead for many years—came to Helen and testified of the truthfulness of all we had taught her—and told Helen that there were many family members waiting for Helen to join the church and do their temple work. When we had knocked on the door earlier, the spirit of her grandmother was still in the room, which is why Helen could not talk to us.

Helen was baptized that evening. I like to think that every member of her family was present—their long wait over.

—*Steve Wernli*

Clearly, It Was True

One day, we were riding our bikes past the church. Occasionally, we would stop at the church to get a drink of water from the fountain or to use the restroom. We did so that day. While we were inside, the phone rang, and I answered it.

It was a man wanting more information about the church. Naturally, we offered to visit his home. He asked if we could come right then. We just happened to be free. Such a thing had never happened to us before, so we rushed on our bikes as fast as we could to the address the man had given to us.

The man greeted us at the door and took us into his library. It was a small room, lined with bookshelves. He told us that he had been searching for a church to join for many years. He explained that he had investigated many different religions and had gathered much information. I had never seen such a collection of books on religion as were shelved in that room.

To our surprise, he had never visited with a member of our church. He wanted to visit with us. We began with a prayer before we taught him the first discussion—which, in those days, was the story of the restoration.

We could tell by the quality of his questions that he was both knowledgeable and teachable—golden. I had to keep pinching myself to see if I was dreaming.

When we completed the discussion, we presented the man with a copy of the Book of Mormon and challenged him to pray about it before he read it.

He was most receptive to that idea. In fact, he had prayed before every book he had ever tried to read on religion. And every time he opened the book, the words blurred before his eyes so that he could not read it.

He was more than anxious to pray before reading the Book of Mormon.

We asked for a second appointment and, once again, he explained his reading procedure to us, adding that, if he were able to read our book, he would call us.

Our hearts sank. Days went by and we did not hear from him. We began to wonder what had happened with our new investigator and the Book of Mormon.

A day or two later, he called. He was most excited and anxious to talk.

He told us that, as soon as we had left his home, he had prayed about our book, and then opened it to read it, and the words were as clear as his eyes had ever read.

While time had separated us, he had read the entire Book of Mormon, and had gained a testimony of its truthfulness, and wondered if we had other books we could read.

We returned with the Doctrine and Covenants and Pearl of Great Price, taught him the second discussion, and challenged him to baptism.

He told us that, as soon as he had read the two new books, he would join the church.

I was transferred the following week, but this man joined the church shortly thereafter.

—*Steve Wernli*

The Starfish

A young man was walking down a deserted beach just before dawn. In the distance he saw a frail old man. As he approached the old man, he watched him pick up a stranded starfish and throw it back into the sea.

The young man gazed in wonder as the old man again and again tossed one small starfish after another from the sand into the water. He asked him, "Why do you expend so much energy doing what seems to be such a waste of time?"

The old man explained that the stranded starfish would die if left in the morning sun.

"But there must be thousands of beaches and millions of starfish," exclaimed the young man. "How can your efforts make any difference?"

The old man looked down at the small starfish in his hand and, as he threw it to safety in the sea, he said, "It makes a difference to this one."

—from Sharon Miller's Missionary Messenger

The church has 11 million members at this writing. There are 6 billion people on the face of the earth at this time. That means that 1/10 of 1 percent of all the people on the earth have the truth—and less than half of them are active. The work before us appears daunting. But, like the starfish, we can make a difference in at least one life, if only our own. And one life can lead to a family, then a community, then a nation, then the world.

Precisely at 9 o'clock

In his book, *The Fire of Faith*, Elder John H. Groberg, writing of his experiences as a mission president in Tonga, shares this lesson:

In Tonga, obedience was understood to be a prerequisite for a mission. As I watched the missionaries, I realized that honest obedience is actually the ultimate expression of faithfulness, for you can't have one without the other.

I was in a store one morning when the store owner looked at a large clock over the door and saw it had stopped during the night. He called to his clerk in the back room and said, "Bill, what time is it? The big clock stopped last night and I need to reset it."

I looked at my watch, but before I could give him the time and before his clerk called back, he suddenly said, "On, never mind, Bill, it's nine o'clock. I can see the Mormon missionaries leaving their fale."

I looked at my watch. It was nine o'clock straight up. I turned to the owner as he was setting the large clock on the wall and asked, "You can set your clock by when the Mormon missionaries leave their house?"

"Of course," he replied. "They always leave at nine o'clock sharp, never a minute before or after. It's one of the things we rely on around here."

I thanked him, completed my business, and then drove a few blocks away to wait for the missionaries to come by. When they arrived, I got out of the car, gave them each a big hug, and thanked them for being so obedient. I said, "You may not know it, but this village sets their clocks by your departure time. Thanks for doing what is right."

They looked at me a little puzzled, almost as if to say, "Well, what did you expect? The mission rule is to be out working at nine o'clock, so of course that is exactly when we leave."

There were other young men remembered for their obedience...two thousand of them, in fact! And they were all young men, and they were exceedingly valiant for courage, and also for strength and activity, but behold, this was not all—they were men who were true at all times in whatsoever thing they were entrusted.
                                                                —*Alma 53:20*

Yea, and they did obey and observe to perform every word of command with exactness.
                                                                —*Alma 57:21*

The Man and the Rock

It happened on a warm spring night.

I was sleeping in my bedroom after a long day of hard work when, suddenly, my bedroom was filled with light and the Savior stood before me.

He said that he had a great work for me to do. Then he showed me a big rock. My work, I learned, was to push the rock with all my strength.

For many days, I tried. I tried hard. Day after day, my shoulders pressed against the cold surface of the rock, pushing with all my strength. And, every night, I retired to my bedroom in the same state: tired, depressed, withered, feeling that my day had been spent in vain.

I started to doubt and began murmuring, "Why am I torturing myself like this? I've been pushing this rock every day and I haven't budged it even one millimeter."

I started to think that my work was impossible, that I wasn't worthy, that I was a useless servant because I couldn't move the rock. These thoughts depressed me, so I started making less of an effort and started murmuring more, "Why do I punish myself like this? I will make only a minimal effort. That will be enough."

Then, I took my problem to the Lord.

"Lord," I said, "I've been working hard for a long time in your service. I've put all my strength into the work you commanded me to do. But, even with my best effort, and after all this time, I couldn't move the rock—not even a millimeter. What's wrong? Why am I failing?"

The Lord answered, "My son, a long time ago when I asked you to serve me, you accepted. I commanded you to push the rock with all your strength,—and, that, you've done.

"Never once did I tell you or expect you to move the rock. The assignment was to push it. And, now, you come to me without strength, convinced that you have failed, and ready to leave your work. But have you really failed?

"Your arms are stronger, your back is strengthened and bronzed from the sun, your hands are calloused from the constant pressure, and your legs are more firm. Through opposition, you have grown. Your ability to overcome is more than before. And, even though you didn't move the rock, you come to me with a broken heart and a body faint.

"My beloved son, I will move the rock. Your work was to be obedient, to push, to exercise faith, and to trust in me—and, that, my beloved son, you have done."

—from Sharon Miller's Missionary Messenger

Planting a Seed

After eight weeks in the MTC, we Romanian-bound missionaries were anxious to get to work.

We boarded our plane to Vienna, Austria, our first stop on the way to Bucharest, Romania, our field of assignment.

When we landed in Vienna, we were anxious to try our newly acquired Romanian language skills, not to mention our newly learned door approach.

So, we missionaries scattered all over the airport in search of someone who spoke Romanian.

We found a Romanian man with his family, also headed to Bucharest. In our broken Romanian, we missionaries did our first door approach, handing the man a Book of Mormon that contained what few excerpts had been translated into Romanian.

The man was taken aback, but graciously accepted the book, and went on his way.

Later, we missionaries were embarrassed by our zeal, and laughed at our awkwardness, not knowing what seed we had planted.

Later, the man sat down and read the excerpts of the Book of Mormon in Romanian. He was intrigued. But, he did not know how to find the missionaries who had given the book to him.

So, using the address inside the book, he wrote a letter to the church in Salt Lake City, who referred him back to the mission office in Budapest, Hungary, who referred him to the missionaries in Bucharest, Romania, who visited, and taught, and baptized him and his family.

We missionaries were not so embarrassed after that. In fact, we increased our door approaches with dramatic results.

—Jayson Fugal

Led by the Spirit

I was in Bucharest, Romania when my mission president called me to be the Zone Leader in Ploesti, a new city the church was just beginning to open up.

I was famous for having too much stuff when it came time to move. Especially via train. The only form of transportation from one city to the next.

Packing and lugging all my stuff to the depot made me and my companion late. We missed our train and had to wait for the next one.

When my companion and I didn't show up at the other end at the prescribed time, the Ploesti missionaries went home without us.

When my companion and I arrived at the other end, there were no local missionaries to greet us, or to escort us to our new apartment.

I didn't know what to do.

Then, again, I did.

I relied on the Spirit.

I had been relying on the Spirit my whole mission.

I had difficulty with the language, but, with the help of the Spirit, I was blessed with the gift of tongues whenever I needed to communicate, or teach, or testify.

Because Romania was a brand new mission, my church materials consisted of a few excerpts from the Book of Mormon translated into Romanian, forcing me to rely on my knowledge and testimony of the gospel, as well as the Spirit, whenever I needed to train, or teach, or testify.

So, when I found myself with no escorts in Ploesti, I relied on the Spirit again.

I hailed a cab and loaded up my companion and all our luggage. I then instructed the cabbie in Romanian, "Start driving."

Like most cabbies worldwide, the cabbie was used to specific directions. But, because I sounded like I knew what I was doing, the cabbie complied.

Every now and then, I instructed the cabbie, "Turn here" or "Turn there". The cabbie did as he was asked.

When we reached a huge complex of government-built apartment buildings, I instructed the cabbie to turn in.

The cabbie did so, creeping along in front of one building after another until I commanded, "Stop here."

My companion and I disembarked, unloaded our luggage, paid the cabbie, and headed into the building, toward the elevator.

The cabbie drove away, surely scratching his head, wondering, I'm sure, what kind of people determine their destination on the fly.

Just as we entered the building, the Ploesti missionaries opened the door.

They were shocked to see me and my companion. And even more shocked to learn how we had gotten there.

But, I wasn't shocked. I had been relying on the Spirit my whole mission.

—*Jayson Fugal*

Putting Things into Perspective

Our oldest son and first missionary, Jayson, was fresh home from his mission to Romania.

His mission had changed him. Tremendously. In more ways than one.

For two years, he had often subsisted on poor food and little heat. He wrote home once, "I am so cold that I don't think I have taken off my overcoat since I got here."

He washed his clothes by jumping up and down on them in the tub.

He stood in food lines like every other Romanian.

He was also called as the branch president of the second branch ever formed in that country—at the tender age of 19, just turning 20.

He did not tell us, not wanting to brag, not wanting us to brag.

His mission president made him call and tell us, so we could pray for him.

We prayed—and then we bragged.

As a branch president, Jayson called the first native Romanian on a mission. He helped prepare the first native Romanians for a temple trip to the temple in Germany. And, he spurred his home teachers to a record-setting 70 percent.

He ate more pig fat than he cared to recount and regularly drank a drink that we would consider curdled milk.

And he taught and baptized people who are the church leaders in Romania today.

His mission changed his life.

So much so, that when he got off the plane, we did not recognize him. He walked right past us and we could not tell it was him—so thin had he gotten, so bad was his haircut, so cheap was his suit, so weird were his glasses.

He thought that was very funny.

We did not.

We had moved into a new home just before Jayson departed on his mission. While he was away, we decorated it. We were anxious to show it off to him. Our dream home.

He walked in, looked around, and said, "It looks like a museum."

I laughed and said, "I quite like the museum look."

He said with contempt, "You need to see how Romanians live."

I stopped showing off.

Christmas was right around the corner. Because it was Jayson's first Christmas home in two years, I went all out with my four trees, two Christmas villages, and half dozen nativities, not to mention exterior lights, and interior parties. It was a grand holiday.

As tradition dictated, on Christmas Eve, we all gathered in the livingroom (one of the few times of year we used the room) for our annual Christmas Eve family home evening. We read the Christmas scriptures, each of our four sons played a favorite Christmas carol on the piano while the rest of us sang, and then each of us shared a favorite Christmas story or thought.

Just as we were about to end, Jayson said, "I want to say something."

We settled back down.

"When I called the first native Romanian on a mission," he said, "I had to meet with his family to see what they could contribute to his mission. They thought long and hard and calculated much before they determined that they could contribute a dollar a month."

We were speechless. I had made a special trip to Hallmark that very day and spent a dollar on one more package of Christmas gift tags so none of our gifts would have to have handmade tags. I was so ashamed of myself.

"We have four Christmas trees," Jayson continued, "and mounds of presents under every one." I shrunk further into my seat. Our other three sons became visibly uncomfortable.

"When my Romanian friends get up tomorrow morning, there will be no Christmas trees. Likely, there will be no gifts. Or food. In fact, most of them have only one pair of shoes."

A long silence followed as we contemplated what he had just said. And we all became a little teary-eyed.

Then my husband Sherm took the lead.

"What can we do?" he asked. "Should we sell everything we have and send the money to Romania?"

We all thought long and hard about that.

Then my husband answered the question himself.

"We are already doing all we can do by raising four sons to serve missions so they can share the gospel with the rest of the world because that is the best thing we have to give and the only thing that will change the world."

We contemplated that thought for a very long time, crying a little more.

And then we knelt in one of the most heart-felt family prayers of our lifetimes together.

It was the most meaningful Christmas Eve we had ever shared. It was the most meaningful family home evening we had ever shared. It was one of the most meaningful moments we had ever shared.

Our three sons followed in Jayson's footsteps and served missions, too. Giving the best thing they had to give and the only thing that will change the world.

—*Peg Fugal*

❦

Called to Serve

When our oldest son Jayson departed on his mission, our youngest son Jer was only 12 years old and a brand new deacon.

One day over lunch, Jer and I were discussing the probability of him also serving a mission. He was hesitant, as only a newly ordained deacon could be.

"I'm afraid," he said.

"Afraid of what?" I asked.

"Afraid God will send me to someplace I can't stand."

I knew I had to address that concern very carefully.

"Jer, you have to trust that God knows you and your abilities and that he will send you to a place that you can stand."

"What if he calls me to China?"

"Then you will learn how to be a missionary in China."

"I can't," he protested. "I can't learn the language, I can't stand the living conditions, I can't eat the food."

"The Lord will help you learn the language and adjust to the lifestyle," I assured him.

He was not convinced.

Several years passed.

Two more brothers went on missions.

Jer's time was approaching. And he was still unsure.

We alerted our home teacher to the problem and he came prepared the next month to address the matter.

"Jer," he began, "do you know how missions calls are made?"

"No," Jer replied, "but I've been wondering about it."

"I knew you were," the home teacher said, "so I did some research on it."

Our home teacher removed his planner from his inside coat pocket, turned a few pages, consulted his notes, and then began.

"When the church receives a potential missionary's papers, they are given to a member of the Church Missionary Committee, who is a General Authority, who sits in front of a computer monitor, which displays all the missions in the world, and indicates which missions need missionaries, and he sits there until he is inspired as to which mission to send that particular missionary."

Jer was very impressed.

So was I.

"Do they ever make mistakes?" Jer ventured.

We were all surprised by the home teacher's reply, "Sometimes."

We watched Jer nervously.

"That's why," the home teacher continued, "the Prophet approves all mission calls. If a mistake in assignment is made, the prophet is inspired to change it."

He then told us a story about just such a thing happening.

Jer was now convinced. Convinced that the Lord knew him. Convinced that, when he was ready, the Lord would know where he was needed to serve. Convinced that, when he got there, the Lord would help him learn the language and adjust to the lifestyle.

Years later, Jer was called to serve in Korea. Though he struggled with the language, he learned it well enough to teach the discussions. Though the living conditions are different, he soon began to enjoy the Korean way of life. Though he generally hates rice and fish, he was soon eating rice and fish with a smile on his face.

—*Peg Fugal*

My Member Missionary Work

As a convert to the church through missionary efforts, I have always taken President McKay's charge—"Every member a missionary"—to heart, seldom failing to share the miracle of the restoration with the non-Mormons around me, seldom hesitating to invite less active members back into the fold. Following are three of my favorite member missionary experiences.

Bringing Betty Back

Betty and her husband joined the church in California. He was a successful businessman; she was a happy homemaker and mother of two lovely daughters and several foster children; they owned a big, beautiful home.

They became great leaders and missionaries in the church in California, opening their hearts and home to everyone and every activity.

Later, they decided to sell their home and move to Utah to be closer to the Saints. They invested the profits from the sale of their home into an LDS-related business, wanting to immerse themselves in Mormonism both personally and professionally.

The business failed—and Betty's health—and attitude—right along with it.

When I met them, they were living in a cramped apartment in a big apartment complex, filled with newlyweds completing school and on their way to something bigger and better—which only added to Betty's misery.

I was assigned to visit teach Betty. I did not like visiting teaching. And, I did not want to visit teach Betty. I had heard her story and I was afraid of her.

My first visit pretty much confirmed my worst fears.

She was in a mood and, before I left, she had attacked nearly every person and program in our ward.

I did not know what to say or do.

I didn't even bother to leave the message.

Then, I avoided her for a couple of months.

Until she called and chastised me for ignoring her.

I returned.

She was in the same foul mood—complaining, complaining, complaining.

I let my mind drift.

I could not go on like this.

I made a point of getting to know her husband, and one of her daughters—who were the complete opposite of Betty—happy, despite their challenges. I wondered why they had not rubbed off on her.

Then, I figured out the problem.

Betty was feeling left out. She had been a major player in the church in California and now she was a failed LDS businesswoman in Utah who she assumed no one wanted anything to do with.

There were lots of activities in the ward and neighborhood, but Betty wasn't invited to any of them—not because people wanted to exclude her—but because everyone was as turned off by her complaining as I was.

I decided to set the example and invited Betty to my next party.

She came dressed up with a smile on her face and could not have been more gracious.

But the next visiting teaching visit was the same old thing—Betty complaining.

It suddenly occurred to me that Betty complained out of habit. Even when things were better, she complained. And there was only one way to stop it.

The next visit, I mustered all my courage to do what had to be done. When Betty started complaining again, I blurted, "Stop it!" Then my face turned red and my heart started pounding.

Betty looked at me wide-eyed.

"Stop complaining," I said. "You have the truth. Remember how you felt when you first learned it and go from there."

She was speechless.

I continued.

"You complain about the leadership of the ward," I said, "instead, ask the Bishop for a calling so you can do your part to improve the ward."

She agreed to do that.

And, I made sure she did it.

"You complain that you have no friends, " I said, "then you befriend someone."

She agreed to do that.

And, I made sure she did it.

"You complain that the church doesn't need you," I said, "but you have a testimony and there are people in this ward who need to hear it."

I had to leave Betty on her own to do that.

But she did. Here a little. There a little.

Pretty soon, Betty was back to being the same active, giving member she had been in California. Pretty soon, she was on everyone's guest list. Pretty soon, she was orchestrating her own activities.

Betty's health failed some more later and things slowed down for her again. But, this time, she did not slip into the complaining mode she had before. This time, she bore her trials with a smile and did her best to stay involved.

Saving Susan

Susan moved into a condo in our ward.

Hers was a tough life. She put her two sons in day care everyday while she worked all day at a wage that hardly made it worth getting out of bed. When she returned home at night, she was so tired that she could barely cope with her sons, let alone all the related responsibilities. Her sons missed their dad and were angry about the divorce. They became more and more challenging to handle. And, when Sunday rolled around, Susan slept in, too tired to cope alone with yet another responsibility.

We were long-time friends of Susan's parents; we had once lived and worked together in the same ward. In fact, I had been one of Susan's Young Women leaders. We were well aware of Susan's heartache. We wanted to help.

My companion and I were assigned to visit teach her; my husband and one of our sons, to home teach her.

Susan welcomed our visits because, "I want my sons to grow up to be just like your sons."

I looked for opportunities to gently point out that our sons had grown up like they did because they were raised in the church. I did not point out that they also had a father.

"I know," she said.

But, when Sundays rolled around, she could not make herself take her sons to church. She was too angry, too hurt, too depressed, too overwhelmed.

Still, we visited.

Month after month.

Year after year.

Leaving a thought, an idea, a little hope, a lot of love every visit.

We watched Susan date one man after another, in search of a new partner, a good father for her sons, most of whom qualified for neither.

And we prayed for her. Prayed that she would come back to church, that she would find the right man to marry, that her heartache would end.

Then she met John. A good man. Going through a divorce himself. With angry children of his own. They were a match made in heaven.

They eventually married. And, with John's help, Susan returned to church.

They have since had two children of their own. And their mixed family gets along better than any of us would ever have predicted.

Some time later, my companion and I ran into Susan, and were surprised by her words.

"I would never have made it if you hadn't kept visiting me," she said. "I needed to know that, even though my life was a disaster, someone loved me."

Following my experiences with both Betty and Susan, I finally figured out what visiting teaching is all about: it is another guise for member missionary work. Which is sometimes as needed as field missionary work. Sometimes more.

Challenging Chris

I knew Chris to be a Mormon: raised in the Church, served a mission. I also knew him to be totally inactive in the church: smoking, drinking, carousing.

I liked Chris. We worked in the same industry. He was one of my favorite suppliers. He was very good at his job. And very good to me. We worked hard and well together, enjoying many business successes, which we celebrated over many business lunches, and some business trips.

Though Chris was careful to live his religion during his work hours, he was not so careful during his free time—which is when I first noticed that he was not living his religion.

I also noticed how unhappy he was. Playing two roles. When he knew which role was his.

Chris was dating a lovely girl. A girl who was also a Mormon. Also inactive. A girl who would have made a great member of the Church. A good LDS wife. And mother.

She had been married before. And been badly hurt. She had a young son. Who very much needed a good LDS father.

She liked Chris. Enjoyed his company. Liked the things he had opened up to her.

Chris loved her. Wanted very much to impress her. And to hold on to her. Wanted very much for her to love him.

But it was a disaster in the making. Two Mormons pretending not to be Mormons. Searching for happiness in all the wrong places.

While traveling abroad with them, watching them handle the inappropriateness of their relationship, watching them shrink whenever another Mormon was present, I decided to speak up.

One night our traveling party was at an Indian restaurant. The food was fabulous. The liquor was flowing. The conversation was riotous. A good time was being had by all. Including me. (Though I was uncomfortable with the liquor and some of the language and stories.)

I watched Chris from a distance. Trying to make sure I, his LDS client, was comfortable, while at the same time, trying to make sure his non-LDS or less active clients were having a good time. It was not working. He was uncomfortable. Embarrassed. A little ashamed of himself.

I leaned over the table and whispered, "Why don't you live what you know to be true?"

That was all I said. He looked at me with a pained expression on his face, shrugged his shoulders, and then turned back to the party.

Some time later, Chris married the girl and became a good father to her son. They had two more children together. They continued to party. Until it was time to take the children to church. Then they visited me. And asked my advice.

"I wouldn't want to raise children in today's world without the armor of God," I answered.

"But, don't you think the church brainwashes people into being automatons?" they asked. Because that was how they had viewed the church in their lives. Or, how they had excused their behavior.

"I think the church is the best training program on the planet for raising responsible adults," I answered.

They contemplated that and then went away.

Some time later, Chris called me on the phone. "We're going to church," he said. That was all.

I asked all about their ward, their callings, their kids' teachers and classmates, their ward activities. All was well.

More time went by.

Then Chris called again. "We're going to the temple," he said. That was all.

I asked all about their temple preparations. All was well.

More time went by.

Then Chris called again. "We're happy," he said. That was all.

I asked all about his life, his wife, his children, his ward, his work. All was well.

More time went by.

Then Chris called again. "I want to thank you for challenging me to live my religion. No one had ever spoken to me like that before. I also want to thank you for loving me even when I wasn't living my religion. Because I'm pretty sure I wouldn't have listened to you had you been judging me."

It was my greatest member missionary moment.

—*Leigh Baugh*

Names in all three stories have been changed for privacy.

❧

My Pen Pal

I once met a handsome, fun-loving, young man who made for an interesting date, but with whom I could never pursue a relationsip.

I had set a goal to marry a returned missionary in the temple. And, though this young man had all the potential in the world, he was clearly not headed in that direction.

Our paths eventually separated.

Three months later, while I was working at a local store, the same young man came in. I called his name and he approached me. I was suddenly very nervous. Though I had not seen him for some time, I was obviously still attracted to him, and I did not know what to say.

"How've you been?" he asked, with his usual cavalier attitude.

"Fine," came my brilliant reply. "I've just been working. What've you been up to?"

"Actually, I'm going on a mission," he replied, with that smile that drove me wild. "I leave for the MTC in two days."

I was so surprised. "Good for you," I said, trying not to sound offensively surprised.

"I'll write to you," he said.

"Oh, sure," I said. Why would he write to me, a girl who had walked away from him.

"No, really, I will," he promised.

"I should be so lucky," I murmured to myself, as he walked away.

Two weeks later, I received a letter in the mail from him. I was more than surprised, I was shocked. I immediately answered it. And, shock of shocks, he wrote again. We became pen pals.

Through his letters, my new pen pal revealed his pre-mission struggles—the pressure he had been under to serve a mission from a family full of missionaries, from a mother who was a convert to the church through missionary efforts.

He wrote that he hadn't wanted to serve a mission just because his dad and brothers had, just because everyone expected it of him; he wanted to serve a mission, only if it was right for him. Meanwhile, he wrote, he was determined to exert his independence by doing what he wanted to do—which included quitting college, working construction, and playing a lot. It wasn't long, he wrote, before he realized how shallow his life had become when compared to the work he might have been doing in the mission field.

Through his letters, he shared two life-changing experiences.

One had happened the previous Christmas when he was visiting his married brother's in-laws out of state. His brother had cornered him one evening in the livingroom after everyone else had gone to bed; the married brother shared his personal testimony of missionary work and challenged my pen pal to serve a mission as well. He wrote that after his brother had left him alone, he suddenly felt enveloped by a dark and menacing presence that scared him half to death.

The next summer, his refusal to serve a mission led to a blow-up with his parents that resulted in him moving out of their home and in with some friends. Some of the friends were also avoiding missions, some had come home from missions early. It was not a good environment.

He asked another married brother if he could move in with him. This wise brother said, "You can live here as long as you are preparing to serve a mission." My pen pal agreed to the condition, with no intentions of following through.

One night, in his basement bedroom, he was once again enveloped by the same dark, menacing presence that had engulfed him the Christmas before. Once again, it scared him half to death.

With his pride finally sapped, he crept out of bed, knelt at his bedside, and prayed. Immediately, the dark presence departed, and the Spirit entered, prompting him to serve a mission.

He had finally received what he had been waiting for: a call. A call to serve a mission—not because others had—not because others expected it—but because it was right for him.

He turned in his missions papers shortly thereafter, received a call a couple of weeks later, and entered the MTC six weeks after that.

His call was to the Orient, a tough mission, with an even tougher language. Though he could easily have become discouraged, he did not. In fact, he was surprisingly positive his whole mission—which was not the young man I had met and dated and parted ways with so long ago. It was the new man we read about in the Book of Mormon:

> *Mosiah 27*
> *25 And the Lord said unto me: Marvel not that all mankind, yea, men and women, all nations, kindreds, tongues and people, must be born again; yea, born of God, changed from their carnal and fallen state, to a state of righteousness, being redeemed of God, becoming his sons and daughters;*
> *26 And thus they become new creatures; and unless they do this, they can in nowise inherit the kingdom of God.*

His last letter, before he became too busy learning and teaching, to write anymore, thanked me for my good influence in his life. I did not know I had influenced him at all. If anything, I had discouraged him, discouraged his wrong choices, which must have somehow encouraged him to make some right choices, the choices that led him to serve the Lord. I was honored to receive a little bit of the credit for his miraculous turnaround.

—*Name withheld*

Thoughts

PHD for a missionary:

P = Prayer

H = Humility

D = Diligence

Dare to be a Mormon,

Dare to stand alone,

Dare to have a purpose,

Dare to make it known.

Every member a missionary!

—David O. McKay

The Lord so loved me that he chose me to serve him.

Be the kind of a companion you would like to be with.

In missionary work, as in all else, preparation precedes power.

—President Gordon B. Hinckley

A mission is not an expense: it is a great investment.

—President Gordon B. Hinckley

Every LDS male who is worthy and able should fill a mission.

—Spencer W. Kimball

You cannot convert people beyond your own conversion.

❧

Put aside every decision of your life until after your mission.

—*Henry D. Moyle*

❧

By going on a mission, we help bridge the gap of the debt we owe the Lord.

❧

Be loyal first to God, the church, and the religion, and second to your companion.

—*Spencer W. Kimball*

❧

Bless us with a desire to reach thy kingdom, and to bring those that we love with us.

—*Rusty Clark*

❧

Pray as if everything depended on the Lord. Work as if everything depended on yourself.

❧

The Lord calls nobody to fail, but to succeed, and this the missionaries should understand fully.

—*Ezra Taft Benson*

❧

You can count the seeds in a single apple, but you can't count the apples in a single seed.

❧

Baptism isn't always the end: we must challenge (warn) the people to make the choice to do the right things.

❧

If God would grant me one wish—just one—it would be this: that each missionary felt and enjoyed the spirit of his calling.

—*Hugh B. Brown*

❧

Every man who has a calling to minister to the inhabitants of the world was ordained to that very purpose in the Grand Council of heaven before this world was.

—*the Prophet Joseph Smith*

Missionary work is the lifeblood of the kingdom. When the blood stops flowing, the kingdom stops growing.

—*Spencer W. Kimball*

You are called upon to declare the words of eternal life with vigor, humility, and faith—bringing out of darkness those who sit in darkness.

—*Joseph Fielding Smith*

If we do not do our duty in regard to missionary service, then I am convinced that God will hold us responsible for the people we might have saved had we done our duty.

—*Spencer W. Kimball*

Missionary work—the preaching of the gospel—has been the major activity of the true Church of Christ whenever the gospel has been upon the earth.

—*Ezra Taft Benson*

A religion that does not require the sacrifice of all things never has power sufficient to produce the faith necessary unto life and salvation.

—*the Prophet Joseph Smith*

Too often we look for big sacrifices—perhaps those that will bring us outside honors—instead of the smaller, more common chances to serve that arise every day.

—*Rulon Dean Skinner*

From now on, from this very moment, you are a trusted representative of your ward, of your parents, and of the Lord Jesus Christ.

—*David O. McKay*

The missionary work of the Latter-day Saints is the greatest of all the great works in all the world.

—Heber J. Grant

❧

We don't ask any people to throw away any good they have got; we only ask them to come and get more.

—the Prophet Joseph Smith

❧

There is no joy that can compare with that of a missionary who has been made the instrument for the salvation of a soul.

—Orson F. Whitney

❧

When missionaries rise to speak in the name of Israel's God, if they live in purity and holiness before him, he will give them words and ideas of which they never dreamed before.

—John Taylor

❧

There is a way to reach every human heart, and it is your business to find the way to the hearts of those to whom you are called on your mission.

—Lorenzo Snow

❧

Let's work! I shall go to my grave saying that missionaries, generally speaking, never rise in their entire life above the stature they carve out for themselves in the mission field.

—Henry D. Moyle

❧

You might prove doctrine from the Bible till doomsday, and it would merely convince a people but would not convert them...nothing short of a testimony by the power of the Holy Ghost would bring light and knowledge to them. Nothing short of that would ever do.

—Brigham Young

❧

We are not justified in waiting for the natural, slow growth which would come with natural and easy proselyting...we believe that we must put our shoulder to the wheel, lengthen our stride, heighten our reach, increase our devotion, so that we can do the work to which we have been assigned.

—Spencer W. Kimball

❧

Come, ye emperors and kings and state leaders, and turn the key. Our missionaries will be powerful ambassadors for your nation. They will bring you peace and joy and a happy, contented people. Please open your doors.

—*Spencer W. Kimball*

❧

They who go forth in the name of the Lord, trusting in him with all their hearts, will never want for wisdom...go in the name of the Lord, trust in the name of the Lord, lean upon the Lord, and call upon the Lord fervently and without ceasing, and pay no attention to the world.

—*Brigham Young*

❧

This call to missionary service does not leave us any choice or option as to the course we should pursue. It is not merely a permissive invitation which allows us to spread the gospel message on a voluntary basis, or if we find it convenient to do so. The decree is mandatory. We have no choice about it, if we are to retain the favor of God.

—*Bruce R. McConkie*

❧

Go in all meekness and sobriety, and preach Jesus Christ and him crucified; not to contend with others on account of their faith, or systems of religion, but to pursue a steady course. This I deliver by way of commandment, and all who observe it not will pull down persecution upon their heads, while those who do shall always be filled with the Holy Ghost; this I pronounce as a prophecy.

—*the Prophet Joseph Smith*

❧

God bless the missionaries wherever they are today, for they are God's servants, as long as they keep themselves pure and spotless from the sins of the world. I testify to you that his Spirit is guiding them, magnifying them in their youth and making them a power in preaching the gospel of Jesus Christ.

—*David O. McKay*

❧

The kind of men we want as bearers of this gospel message are men who have faith in God, men who have faith in their religion, men who honor their priesthood, in whom God has confidence. Men who bear the words of life among the nations ought to be men of honor, integrity, virtue, and purity; and this being the command of God to us, we shall try to carry it out.

—*John Taylor*

❧

Go forth and preach the gospel, gain an experience, learn wisdom and walk humbly before your God, that you may receive the Holy Ghost to guide you and direct you and teach you all things past, present, and to come. Go trusting in God, and continue to trust in him and he will open your way and multiply upon you.

—*Brigham Young*

The first great commandment is to love the Lord our God with all our hearts, might, mind, and strength: and the second is like unto it, to love our neighbors as ourselves. And the best way in the world to show our love for our neighbor is to go forth and proclaim the gospel of the Lord Jesus Christ, of which he has given us an absolute knowledge concerning its divinity.

—*Heber J. Grant*

One of the greatest secrets of missionary work is work. If a missionary works, he will get the Spirit; if he gets the Spirit, he will teach by the Spirit; and, if he teaches by the Spirit, he will touch the hearts of the people—and he will be happy. There will be no homesickness, no worrying about families—for all time and talents and interests are centered on the work of the ministry. That's the secret—work, work, work. There is no satisfactory substitute, especially in missionary work.

—*Ezra Taft Benson*

If you go on a mission to preach the gospel with lightness and frivolity in your hearts, looking for this and that, and to learn what is in the world, and not having your minds riveted—yes, I say riveted—on the cross of Christ, you will go and return in vain. Let your minds be centered on your missions and labor earnestly to bring souls to Christ.

—*Brigham Young*

Your mission is preparation. It is your school for eternity. You won't forget that, will you? This mission is not just a two-year stretch. This is the time when you cultivate the seeds of Godhood so that you can help other people on their way toward exaltation. How small are we who think of the mission as just being a stretch of time, some physical things to do, a little studying to do, some praying. This is the most purposeful thing, perhaps, you have ever done in your life—and, possibly, the most purposeful thing that some of you will ever do. It's up to you to let this be the prelude to your life, to let it be the beginning of a great and glorious life.

—*Spencer W. Kimball*

Feast on His Words

And they said one to another, Did not our heart burn within us, while he talked with us by the way, and while he opened to us the scriptures?
—*Luke 24:32*

Then opened he their understanding, that they might understand the scriptures,
—*Luke 24:45*

Angels speak by the power of the Holy Ghost; wherefore, they speak the words of Christ. Wherefore, I said unto you, feast upon the words of Christ; for behold, the words of Christ will tell you all things what ye should do.
—*2 Nephi 32:3*

Studying the scriptures is one of the great keys to spiritual success and, somehow, we must learn to love them.

Learning to love the scriptures is no different from learning to love anything else. We must practice, practice, practice, and then practice some more.

Never would we attempt to play in a major sports championship, or play an instrument in a recital, without having practiced many hours.

Yet, many feel they can unlock the excitement and beauty of the scriptures by reviewing them for only a few minutes a week. It doesn't work that way.

Of course, snacking is better than starving, but the Lord admonishes us to "feast on his words." Then, when we savor them, and digest them, they become a part of us, and give life.

—*Jack Christianson*

༻✺༺

10 Commandments of Missionary Conduct

1. Thou shalt give thyself fully to the work.

2. Thou shalt observe the safety rule of always going everywhere with your companion.

3. Thou shalt write no letter to any local sister, or socialize with any girls.

4. Thou shalt bend both thy knees.

5. Thou shalt love the Lord and thy fellow man.

6. Thou shalt develop humility in all its finer aspects.

7. Thou shalt be absolutely truthful and honest.

8. Thou shalt develop faith all the days of thy mission.

9. Thou shalt follow the schedule absolutely and meticulously.

10. Thou shalt be immediately obedient.

༻✺༺

The Standard of Truth

The standard of truth has been erected. No unhallowed hand can stop the work from progressing; persecutions may rage, mobs may combine, armies may assemble, calumny may defame, but the truth of God will go forth boldly, nobly and independent, until it has penetrated every continent, visited every climb, swept every country and sounded forth in every ear, until the purposes of God shall be accomplished and the Great Jehovah shall say the work is done.

—the Prophet Joseph Smith

Standards Are Important!

If you think giving less than 100 percent will do, then consider what happens when only 99.9 percent is given in these instances:

—2 airplane landings will be unsafe at Chicago's O'Hare International Airport

—12 babies will be given to the wrong parents

—55 malfunctioning ATMs will be installed in the next 12 months

—107 incorrect medical procedures will be performed by the end of the day

—291 pacemaker operations will be performed incorrectly this year

—315 entries will turn out to be misspelled in *Webster's Third New International Dictionary of the English Language*

—1,314 telephone calls will be misplaced by telecommunications services every minute

—3,056 copies of tomorrow's *Wall Street Journal* will be missing a section

—$9,690 will be spent on defective, often unsafe, sports equipment

—14,208 defective PCs will be shipped this year

—18,322 pieces of mail will be mishandled in the next hour

—20,000 incorrect drug prescriptions will be written in the next 12 months

—22,000 checks will be deducted from the wrong bank accounts in the next hour

—103,260 income tax returns will be processed incorrectly this year

—114,500 mismatched pairs of shoes will be shipped in the next year

—268,000 defective tires will be shipped this year

—$761,900 will be spent in the next 12 months on CDs and tapes that won't play

—811,000 faulty rolls of 35 mm film will be loaded this year

—880,000 credit cards in circulation will turn out to have incorrect cardholder information on their magnetic strips

—2,000,000 documents will be lost by the IRS this year

—2,488,200 books will be shipped with the wrong cover in the next 12 months

—5,517,200 cases of soft drinks produced in the next 12 months will be flatter than a bad tire

Can you live with 99.9 percent?

✌

The Values of Life

The Greatest Handicap...Fear

The Best Day...Today

The Hardest Thing...To Begin

The Easiest Thing...Finding Fault

The Most Useless Asset...Pride

The Most Useful Asset...Humility

The Greatest Mistake...Giving Up

The Greatest Stumbling Block...Egotism

The Greatest Comfort...Work Well Done

The Most Disagreeable Person...The Complainer

The Worst Bankruptcy...Loss of Enthusiasm

The Greatest Need...Common Sense

The Meanest Feeling...Regret at Another's Success

The Best Gift...Forgiveness

The Hardest To Accept...Defeat

The Greatest Moment...Death

The Greatest Knowledge...God

The Greatest Thing...Love

The Greatest Success...Self-Fulfillment and Peace of Mind

✌

The Incomparable Christ

More than nineteen hundred years ago there was a man born contrary to the laws of life.

He lived in poverty and was reared in obscurity; he received no formal education and never possessed wealth or widespread influence.

He never traveled extensively; in fact, he crossed the boundary of his own country only once.

But this man's life has changed the course of history.

In infancy, he started out as a king; in childhood, he confounded intellects; in manhood, he ruled nature, walking upon the waves, and calming the sea.

He healed multitudes without medicine or charge for his services.

He never practiced psychiatry, yet he has healed more broken hearts than all the doctors that ever lived.

He never wrote a book, yet his life has inspired more books than any other man.

He never wrote a song, yet his life has inspired far more songs than all other song writers combined.

He never founded a college, yet all the schools added together cannot boast such an alumni.

He never marshaled an army, or drafted a soldier, or fired a gun, yet no leader has ever had more people surrender their lives to him without firing a shot.

The names of great statesmen have come and gone. Scientists, philosophers, and theologians are soon forgotten. But the name of this man abounds forevermore.

Once each week the wheels of commerce cease their turning and multitudes gather to pay homage and respect to him.

Though time has put two thousand years between this generation and his birth, he still lives. His enemies could not destroy him, and the grave could not hold him.

This man stands forth upon the highest pinnacle of heavenly glory, proclaimed of God, acknowledged by angels, adored by his people, and feared by devils, as the risen Lord and Savior, Jesus Christ.

—Jim Bishop

The Chinese Bamboo Tree

Zig Zigler, the noted motivational speaker, tells the story of the Chinese bamboo tree.

The first year, the Chinese plant the seed, and water and fertilize it, but nothing happens.

The second year, they water and fertilize it more, and nothing happens.

The third year, they continue watering and fertilizing it, and nothing happens.

The fourth year, they water and fertilize it some more, and, still, nothing happens.

The fifth year, they continue watering and fertilizing it, and, sometime in the course of that year, in a period of only six weeks, the Chinese bamboo tree suddenly and most miraculously sprouts to a gigantic 90 feet!

The question is: did the Chinese bamboo tree grow 90 feet in six weeks, or did it grow 90 feet over five years?

The answer is obvious: it grew 90 feet over five years—because had the Chinese not watered or fertilized the seed any one of those years, then there would be no Chinese bamboo tree at all.

The same can be said of LDS missionaries who grow so tall spiritually during the two years of their service.

The question is: did they grow so tall spiritually in two years, or did they grow so tall spiritually over a lifetime?

The answer is obvious: they grew so tall spiritually over a lifetime—because had they and their family and their church leaders and teachers and the Spirit not watered and fertilized their faith any one of those years, then there would be no LDS missionaries at all.

Alma's great discourse on faith to the Zoramites makes the same point. And, it applies to both missionaries, as well as their investigators:

Alma 32

26 Now, as I said concerning faith—that it was not a perfect knowledge—even so it is with my words. Ye cannot know of their surety at first, unto perfection, any more than faith is a perfect knowledge.

27 But behold, *if ye will awake and arouse your faculties,* even to an *experiment upon my words,* and *exercise a particle of faith,* yea, even if ye can no more than desire to believe, *let this desire work in you,* even *until ye believe* in a manner that ye can *give place for a portion of my words.*

28 Now, we will *compare the word unto a seed.* Now, *if ye give place, that a seed may be planted in your heart,* behold, *if it be a true seed, or a good seed, if ye do not cast it out* by your unbelief, that ye will resist the Spirit of the Lord, behold, *it will begin to swell within your breasts;* and *when you feel these swelling motions, ye will begin to say* within yourselves—*It must needs be that this is a good seed, or that the word is good, for it beginneth to enlarge my soul; yea, it beginneth to enlighten my understanding, yea, it beginneth to be delicious to me.*

29 Now behold, would not this increase your faith? I say unto you, Yea; *nevertheless it hath not grown up to a perfect knowledge.*

30 But behold, *as the seed swelleth, and sprouteth, and beginneth to grow, then you must needs say that the seed is good*; for behold it swelleth, and sprouteth, and beginneth to grow. And now behold, will not this strengthen your faith? *Yea, it will strengthen your faith*: for ye will say I know that this is a good seed; for behold it sprouteth and beginneth to grow.

31 And now, behold, *are ye sure that this is a good seed?* I say unto you, *Yea; for every seed bringeth forth unto its own likeness.*

32 Therefore, *if a seed groweth it is good, but if it groweth not, behold it is not good,* therefore it is cast away.

33 And now, behold, because ye have tried the experiment, and planted the seed, and it swelleth and sprouteth, and beginneth to grow, ye must needs know that the seed is good.

34 And now, behold, *is your knowledge perfect? Yea, your knowledge is perfect in that thing, and your faith is dormant*; and this because ye know, for ye know that the word hath swelled your souls, and ye also know that it hath sprouted up, that your understanding doth begin to be enlightened, and your mind doth begin to expand.

35 O then, *is not this real?* I say unto you, *Yea, because it is light; and whatsoever is light, is good, because it is discernible,* therefore ye must know that it is good; and now behold, *after ye have tasted this light is your knowledge perfect?*

36 Behold I say unto you, *Nay; neither must ye lay aside your faith, for ye have only exercised your faith to plant the seed* that ye might try the experiment to know if the seed was good.

37 And behold, *as the tree beginneth to grow*, ye will say: Let us *nourish it with great care, that it may get root, that it may grow up, and bring forth fruit* unto us. And now behold, if ye nourish it with much care it will get root, and grow up, and bring forth fruit.

38 But *if ye neglect the tree*, and take no thought for its nourishment, behold it will not get any root; and when the heat of the sun cometh and scorcheth it, because it hath no root *it withers away, and ye pluck it up and cast it out.*

39 Now, *this is not because the seed was not good*, neither is it because the fruit thereof would not be desirable; but *it is because your ground is barren*, and ye will not nourish the tree, therefore ye cannot have the fruit thereof.

40 And thus, *if ye will not nourish the word, looking forward with an eye of faith to the fruit thereof, ye can never pluck of the fruit of the tree of life.*

41 But *if ye will nourish the word*, yea, nourish the tree as it beginneth to grow, *by your faith with great diligence, and with patience, looking forward to the fruit thereof, it shall take root; and behold it shall be a tree springing up unto everlasting life.*

42 And because of your diligence and your faith and your patience with the word in nourishing it, that it may take root in you, behold, *by and by ye shall pluck the fruit thereof, which is most precious, which is sweet above all that is sweet, and which is white above all that is white, yea, and pure above all that is pure; and ye shall feast upon this fruit even until ye are filled, that ye hunger not, neither shall ye thirst.*

43 *Then, my brethren, ye shall reap the rewards of your faith, and your diligence, and patience, and long-suffering,* waiting for the tree to bring forth fruit unto you.

—*from Sharon Miller's Missionary Messenger*

❧

The Biggest Mathematical Miracle in the World

Getting 2 million Israelites out of Egypt was one thing; caring for 2 million people in the desert for 40 years was quite another.

According to the U.S. Army Quartermaster General, to feed 2 million people, Moses would have had to procur 1,500 tons of food every day—which, today, would require two freight trains—each 1 mile long.

To cook the food would require 4,000 tons of firewood a day—nearly 3 freight trains—each 1 mile long!

To drink and wash would require 11 million gallons of water a day—which, today, would require a freight train of tanker cars 1,000 miles long.

Then, there was the problem of crossing the Red Sea.

If the Israelites walked 2 abreast on a narrow path through the sea, the path would have been more than 800 miles long, and it would have required 35 days and nights to walk 2 million people across it. The Israelites were being pursued by the Egyptians: they had only 1 evening to cross the Red Sea. So, the path had to be 3 miles wide and the Israelites had to walk 5,000 abreast.

And then there was the problem of camping.

A campsite of 2 million Israelites would be roughly 2/3 the size of the state of Rhode Island—or 750 square miles—every night as they progressed along their route to the promised land—for more than 40 years.

Do you think Moses took the time or had the ability to calculate and prepare for all of the above before escaping the wrath of Egypt? Of course not! Moses and the Israelites were led by God in a cloud during the day and in a fire by night. God took care of the details.

The same thing happened when Brigham Young led thousands of Saints out of Nauvoo and across the great plains and through the Rocky Mountains into the great basin.

With all that in mind, do you actually think God cannot take care of you and your needs and your problems? Of course not! You need only to follow him day and night.

❧

A Lesson from the Geese

Point 1: As each bird flaps its wings, it creates an uplift for the bird following. By flying in a v-formation, the whole flock adds 71 percent more flying range than if each bird flew alone.

Lesson: People who share a common direction and sense of community can get where they are going quicker and easier because they are traveling on the thrust of one another.

Point 2: Whenever a goose falls out of formation, it suddenly feels the drag and resistance of trying to fly alone, and quickly gets back into formation to take advantage of the lifting power of the birds immediately in front.

Lesson: If we have as much sense as a goose, we will go in formations with those who are headed where we want to go.

Point 3: When the lead goose gets tired, it rotates back into the formation and another goose flies at the point position.

Lesson: It pays to take turns doing the hard tasks, and sharing leadership with people, as with geese, interdependent with each other.

Point 4: The geese in formation honk from behind to encourage those up front to keep up their speed.

Lesson: We need to make sure our honking from behind is encouraging—not something less helpful.

Point 5: When a goose gets sick or wounded or shot down, two geese drop out of the formation and follow their fellow member down to help and provide protection. They stay with this member of the flock until he or she is either able to fly again or dies. Then, they launch out on their own with another formation or to catch up with their own flock.

Lesson: If we have as much sense as the geese, we'll stand by each other, too.

—*Meile W. Boos*

The Christus Presentation

When visitors to Temple Square in Salt Lake City visit the Christus statue surrounded by the heavens in the rotunda of the North Visitor's Center, they hear the following recording, as though Christ himself were speaking:

3 Nephi 9

15 Behold, I am Jesus Christ...I created the heavens and the earth, and all things that in them are. I was with the Father from the beginning...

3 Nephi 27

13 ...I came into the world to do the will of my Father...
14 ...my Father sent me that I might be lifted up upon the cross...that I might draw all men unto me...

Doctrine and Covenants 19

23 Learn of me, and listen to my words; walk in the meekness of my Spirit, and you shall have peace in me.

Doctrine and Covenants 6

37 Behold the wounds which pierced my side, and also the prints of the nails in my hands and feet...

Doctrine and Covenants 19

16 For behold, I...have suffered these things for all, that they might not suffer if they would repent;

John 14

1 Let not your heart be troubled: ye believe in God, believe also in me.

John 13

34 A new commandment I give unto you, That ye love one another; as I have loved you, that ye also love one another.
35 By this shall all [men] know that ye are my disciples...

John 14

2 In my Father's house are many mansions...I go to prepare a place for you.

John 14

15 If ye love me, keep my commandments.

❧

17 Heretofore Unknown or Forgotten Truths Revealed by The First Vision:

1. Prayers are heard and answered

2. Satan is real

3. Satan has power over us

4. Satan wants to thwart good

5. Satan wants to stop the truth

6. Satan cannot abide the presence of the Father or the Son

7. The Father and the Son have power over Satan

8. The heavens are not closed, revelation has not ceased

9. Miracles have not ceased

10. The Father and the Son are two separate beings

11. The Father and the Son have bodies of flesh and bone

12. The Father introduces the Son, the Son is the spokesman for the Father

13. No other church is true

14. Joseph Smith is a prophet, called by God

15. Joseph Smith and the prophets are the mouth-pieces of the Lord

16. The promised restoration has begun

17. The final dispensation of the Fullness of Times is underway

⸙

Our Thinking vs. God's Promises

IT'S IMPOSSIBLE!
All things are possible.

—Luke 18:27

I'M TOO TIRED.
I will give you rest.

—Matthew 11:28-30

NOBODY REALLY LOVES ME.
I love you.

—John 3:16 & John 13:34

I CAN'T GO ON!
My grace is sufficient.

—2 Corinthians 12:9 & Psalm 9 1:15

I CAN'T FIGURE THINGS OUT!
I will direct your steps.

—Proverbs 3:5-6

I CAN'T DO IT!
You can do all things.

—Phillipians 4:13

I'M NOT ABLE!
I am able.

—2 Corinthians 9:8

IT'S NOT WORTH IT!
It will be worth it.

—Romans 8:28

I CAN'T FORGIVE MYSELF.
I forgive you.

—1 John 1:9 & Romans 8:1

I CAN'T MANAGE!
I will supply all your needs.

—Phillipians 4:19

I'M AFRAID.
I have not given you a spirit of fear.

—2 Timothy 1:7

I'M ALWAYS WORRIED AND FRUSTRATED!
Cast all your cares on me.

—1 Peter 5:7

I DON'T HAVE ENOUGH FAITH.
I've given everyone a measure of faith.

—Romans 12:3

I'M NOT SMART ENOUGH!
I give you wisdom.

—1 Corinthians 1:30

I FEEL ALL ALONE.
I will never leave you or forsake you.

—Hebrews 13:5

⚘

The Epistle of the Missionaries to the Letter-Writers

Chapter 1

1. In the beginning was the mailbox, and the mailbox was void of letters.

2. And the missionaries said, "Let the box be filled," and the box was not filled.

Chapter 2

1. And we give unto you the parable of the two letter-writers.

2. At the hour of noon, a certain scribe sat down to write a letter.

3. And the scribe did think of many things to write, but lo, he spent so much time thinking that he did not write.

4. Nevertheless, he felt good because of his intentions.

5. At the same hour, a publican sat down and wrote a few words as he ate.

6. Yet, he felt guilty at not writing more.

7. And lo, two years did pass and the missionary returned home, and passed by the scribe's house.

8. Yea, he went even unto the house of the publican and did visit the publican.

Chapter 3

1. And if you should spend but five minutes writing one letter to a missionary, how great shall be your joy.

2. And if your joy be great with one letter, how great shall be your joy with many letters in the mailbox of a missionary.

3. Else why did they build post offices if letters are written not at all; why then do they build post offices?

Chapter 4

1. But some will say, "A letter! A letter! We have already written a letter. What need have we to write any more letters?"

2. Know ye not that there are more days than one? And more events in a day? Why think ye that those events need not be reported?

Chapter 5

1. And we give unto you the parable of the self-addressed-stamped envelopes.

2. When a missionary departed unto a far-off land, he gave a certain number of self-addressed-stamped envelopes to his friends.

3. Unto one he gave five, and unto another he gave two, and unto another he gave one.

4. And while he was gone, he that was given five envelopes wrote five letters and then in zeal wrote five more.

5. The same with him that had been given two envelopes; he wrote two letters and then two more.

6. But, he that was given one self-addressed-stamped envelope became slothful and careless, and lost the envelope, even that which he was given.

7. And when the missionary came home, he went unto his friends.

8. And he that had written ten letters was warmly greeted; the same with he that had written four.

9. But, he that had written none at all was given nothing more than a fish-like handshake.

❧

The Missionary

Somewhere between the whirl of the teenage activity and the confinement of rocking chair, we find a strange creature called a missionary.

Missionaries come in two varieties—Elders and Sisters—who come in different sizes, weights, and colors—green being the most common.

Converts love them, young girls worship them (the Elder variety), dogs hate them, the law tolerates them, most people ignore them, and heaven protects them.

A missionary is truth with a pocket full of tracts, wisdom with a scant knowledge of the Bible, faith with 69 cents in his pocket and two weeks until dad's next check.

A missionary is a composite. He has the appetite of a horse, the enthusiasm of a fire cracker, the patience of Job, the persistence of the fuller brush man, and the courage of a lion tamer.

He likes letters from home, invitations to Sunday dinners, conferences, checks, testimony meetings, companions, baptisms, and visits from the Mission President.

He isn't much on tracting in the rain, people who slam doors, helmets, apartment houses, transfers, shaking hands at arm's length, alarm clocks, and, last but not least, letters that start with "Dear John".

Nobody rises so early or is so tired by 10:30 p.m. Nobody else can knock so boldly with such a shaky hand. Nobody else can get such a thrill at the end of a disappointing day, when someone says, "Won't you come in, we've been waiting for you!"

Yes, a missionary is a queer character. He can get homesick, and temporarily lose faith in the human race, but a strange lump rises in his throat the day he receives his letter of release and, upon arrival at home, his homecoming talk will probably contain the phrase once considered trite, "It was the best two years of my life."

—*Dan Valentine*

❧

The Missionary's Girl

Somewhere between the whirl of teen-age dates and the responsibility of matrimony, we find a lone creature called the missionary's girl.

They come in two varieties—engaged and hopefuls. They come in assorted sizes, weights, and colors—blue being the most common.

The missionary's girl is found at home, missing parties, staying away from dances, paying her own way to the movies, buying stationery by the gross.

Missionaries love them, young girls look up to them, parents tolerate them, postmen hate them, and weekly letters support them.

A missionary's girl is a composite. She has the appetite of a mouse, the enthusiasm of a wet noodle, the patience of Job, the persistence of a stainless steel salesman, and the imagination of Scherazade.

She likes letters from the mission field, invitations to his home, long distance telephone calls, items for his scrapbook, pictures of him, and other girls who are waiting.

She isn't much for Saturday nights at home; people who say, "two years is a long time"; new clothes with no one to wear them for; sad movies and music; movies with love scenes; knitting; wedding receptions; little sisters who date; calendars; and "Dear Janes".

A missionary's girl is an odd object. She can get lonesome, discouraged, and temporarily lose faith in the whole missionary system. No one else can write such cheerful letters in such a rotten mood. No one else can get such a thrill at the end of the day by the words, "Why, yes, I believe there is a letter for you." Nobody else is so early to bed and so early to rise.

A missionary's girl is virtue with no chance to be otherwise, faith with twenty-four months to wait, prudence with 69 cents in her savings account, and beauty with no one to give a darn.

Yes, she is all this, but it will all be forgotten the day he receives his letter of release and, upon his arrival home, she will probably utter the words she once considered trite, "It hasn't seemed like any time at all!"

—Dan Valentine

Afterword

We cannot conclude without mentioning our Utah Valley neighbor, Elder Orin Vorheis, who lies in a hospital bed in his parents' home in Pleasant Grove, following a gunshot wound to the head, sustained while serving in the Argentina Buenos Aires South Mission.

Though Elder Voorheis has received tremendous medical attention, he is paralyzed and cannot speak. His communication is limited to a few hand movements.

Members of Elder Vorheis' ward and stake regularly visit to help with his physical therapy, which is demanding work—Elder Vorheis is a big missionary.

Visitors always note that Elder Vorheis still wears his missionary nametag, though he has been home from his mission for some time now. Elder Vorheis will continue to wear his nametag until he is able to report his mission to his Stake President, or a higher authority.

Though you would expect to find a family embittered by the tragedy suffered by their missionary, you will not. They are proud of Elder Vorheis' missionary service and they work tirelessly caring for a body scarred during that service.

Elder Vorheis and his family are some of the church's greatest missionaries. We conclude this work by honoring them.

Index

Other books in this series:
The Best of Especially for Mormons
Christmas Especially for Mormons

Other *Especially for Mormons* products:
The Best of Especially for Mormons on Audiocassette
The Original Five Volumes of Especially for Mormons on CD-ROM

Especially for Mormon Women:
Our fourth volume, *Especially for Mormon Women*, will be released Christmas 2002. We invite you to submit pieces you would like to see included by simply emailing the piece to me at pegfugal@aol.com anytime before the end of July 2002. (I am sorry, but we cannot accept material in any other way.)